5th October 2007

Mummy and Daddy,

Thank you so much for the last two weeks.
I'm so grateful for everything, especially all
the delicious food and wine! Here is something
to remember Australia by (until next time!) -
the photos and the tastes!

I love you very much,

Nina
xxx

simply australia

A CULINARY JOURNEY

simply australia

A CULINARY JOURNEY

NEW
HOLLAND

Published in Australia by
New Holland Publishers (Australia) Pty Ltd
Sydney • Auckland • London • Cape Town
14 Aquatic Drive Frenchs Forest NSW 2086 Australia
218 Lake Road Northcote Auckland New Zealand
24 Nutford Place London W1H 6DQ United Kingdom
80 McKenzie Street Cape Town 8001 South Africa

First published in 1997 by
Chanel Publishers T/A C. J. Publishing
Reprinted in 1999 by
New Holland Publishers (Australia) Pty Ltd

National Library of Australia
Cataloguing-in-Publication Data:

Simply Australia: a culinary journey.

Includes index.
ISBN 1 86436 575 7

1. Cookery - Australia. 2. Australia - Description and
travel. I. Ryan II. Baker, Ian.

641.5994

acknowledgements

In the course of producing this book we visited many areas which were not well known to us. We extend a warm thank you to those who guided us around Australia to achieve what we consider to be a good representation of Australian Cuisine. We also extend a thank you to TRANZ/Photo Index for providing some excellent scenic pictures.

A special thanks to Ian Baker for his enthusiasm in completing the recipe photography and help in collecting the recipes.

To Jan Bilton, Michael Ryan, Pamela Parsons and Mary Dobbyn a sincere thank you for putting together a wonderful publication. Special mention goes to Dexter Fry for his superb design and production. Most of all, our thanks to the owner and chefs of the Australian restaurants participating in this culinary journey.

Publisher: Cliff Josephs
Text: Michael Ryan
Editor: Pamela Parsons
Food Editor: Jan Bilton
Editorial Assistant: Mary Dobbyn
Design and Production: Dexter Fry
Cover design: Mark Thacker
Photography: Ian Baker and contributors, with the exception of the following: NHIL/ Shaen Adey, title and imprint pages; NHIL/ Anthony Johnson, cover (top)
Printed by Bookbuilders, Hong Kong

CONTENTS

INTRODUCTION

Few countries in the world can offer the variety, quality and sheer creativity found in Australian restaurants. *Simply Australia* takes you on the gourmet trail around a vast continent packed with culinary and scenic surprises. Each state or region vies to create distinctive cuisine and each has its own acknowledged specialities. The quality and originality of the food is remarkable.

The selection facing our photographer, Ian Baker, was vast, and he had some difficult choices to make! We were delighted with the warm reception we received from the contributing chefs and thank them sincerely for taking the time to prepare tempting examples of the dishes that have delighted their clientele. Regrettably, some very fine establishments were omitted due to scheduling conflicts. We hope to include them in a future edition.

Some of the recipes have been adapted slightly to ensure they are easy to follow. You will find a wide assortment of delicious and fascinating styles like Pink Peppercorn and Mustard Seed Marinade for Pearl Meat (from Broome) and Char-grilled Kangaroo with a Roasted Mushroom and Hunter Sauce (from Darwin).

Combining creative cooking and magnificent photography, *Simply Australia* is simply different — both a gourmet's guide to travel and a traveller's guide to gourmet delights.

Cliff Josephs
Publisher

The photographs on the previous pages are: (2-3) Australian countryside, (4-5) Whitsundays, (6-7) Great Barrier Reef, (8-9) Bungle Bungle. The map on the facing page is a state by state guide to our culinary journey.

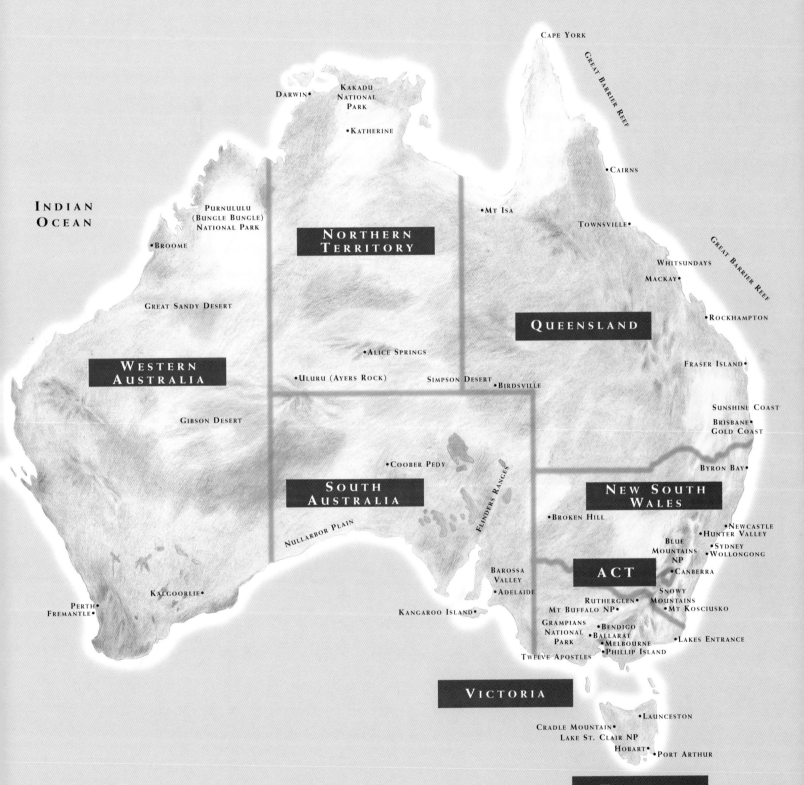

PACIFIC
OCEAN

CAPE YORK

GREAT BARRIER REEF

DARWIN• KAKADU
NATIONAL
PARK

•KATHERINE

•CAIRNS

INDIAN
OCEAN

PURNULULU
(BUNGLE BUNGLE)
NATIONAL PARK

•Mt ISA

TOWNSVILLE•

•BROOME

NORTHERN
TERRITORY

WHITSUNDAYS
MACKAY•

GREAT BARRIER REEF

GREAT SANDY DESERT

QUEENSLAND

•ROCKHAMPTON

WESTERN
AUSTRALIA

•ALICE SPRINGS

•ULURU (AYERS ROCK)

SIMPSON DESERT
•BIRDSVILLE

FRASER ISLAND•

GIBSON DESERT

SUNSHINE COAST

BRISBANE•
GOLD COAST

•COOBER PEDY

BYRON BAY•

SOUTH
AUSTRALIA

FLINDERS RANGES

NEW SOUTH
WALES

•BROKEN HILL

•NEWCASTLE
•HUNTER VALLEY
BLUE
MOUNTAINS
NP

NULLARBOR PLAIN

•SYDNEY
•WOLLONGONG

ACT

•CANBERRA

KALGOORLIE•

BAROSSA
VALLEY

SNOWY
MOUNTAINS

RUTHERGLEN•

•Mt KOSCIUSKO

PERTH•
FREMANTLE•

•ADELAIDE

Mt BUFFALO NP•

KANGAROO ISLAND•

GRAMPIANS
NATIONAL
PARK

•BENDIGO
•BALLARAT
•MELBOURNE
•PHILLIP ISLAND

•LAKES ENTRANCE

TWELVE APOSTLES

VICTORIA

•LAUNCESTON

CRADLE MOUNTAIN
LAKE ST. CLAIR NP

HOBART• •PORT ARTHUR

TASMANIA

NEW SOUTH WALES

WHEN THE SURF is booming along the golden beaches of the east, dust storms can be swirling across the arid west. When monsoonal rains are sweeping the rainforests of the north, snow can be falling on the ski fields of the south. New South Wales, Australia's most populous state, is a tapestry of contrasts and surprises. And so is Sydney (pictured) Australia's oldest and largest city.

Dazzling, vibrant, sitting majestically on the shores of one of the world's great harbours, Sydney has come a long way from her unhappy beginnings as a penal colony on the edge of an alien land. Home to nearly four million people, this brash, bustling metropolis never ceases to surprise — 34 surfing beaches including Bondi (see page 14) which attracts thousands; a world-class Opera House; one of the country's most sumptuous shopping centres, the Byzantine Queen Victoria Building which takes up an entire block; the world's most pleasant form of commuter transport — the harbour ferries; the award-winning Powerhouse Museum that explores almost every realm of human creativity; and of course the extraordinary restaurant scene — eating out is one of the great delights of Sydney.

CONFIT OF GREENLIP ABALONE WITH BLACK FUNGI, NOODLE SALAD & TRUFFLE OIL DRESSING

1 kg Greenlip abalone alive in the shell
extra virgin olive oil (preferably Colonna)
6 pieces star anise
1 knob of ginger, peeled and finely sliced

NOODLE SALAD

2 tablespoons mushroom soy sauce
¼ cup truffle-infused extra virgin olive oil
300 g extra-fine hand-made egg noodles,
blanched and cooked in water
50 g each black fungus, white fungus,
shiitake mushrooms, julienned
50 g Enjoki mushrooms, washed
and separated
30 g Ogo Nori (salted fresh green seaweed)
3 cm piece young ginger, julienned
2 spring onions, julienned
50 g fresh ocean trout roe
pepper

To prepare the abalone, remove from shell. Scrape all the colouring and intestine until all the flesh is white. Cook at 60°C for 3 hours in extra virgin olive oil, star anise and ginger. Use a baking pan just large enough to fit the abalone. The abalone must be covered completely in olive oil. To prepare the noodle salad, combine mushroom soy and truffle oil to make a light dressing. Lightly dress the noodles and combine with other salad ingredients, place salad in the centre of 4 plates.Once the abalone has cooked slice it into paper-thin slices and divide evenly between the plates. Finish with ground pepper and a little more truffle oil. Serves 4.

ROCKPOOL, SYDNEY, NEW SOUTH WALES.

Roast Crown of Hare on a Gateau of Cabbage & Oriental Mushrooms With a Cepe Mushroom Sauce

POMMES DAUPHIN
3 large potatoes
salt and pepper
butter for cooking

CEPE MUSHROOM SAUCE
50 g shallots, chopped
¼ cup each port wine, Madeira
50 g dried cepe mushrooms
½ cup hare jus
1¾ cups cream
salt and pepper

CROWN ROAST
oil
salt and pepper
2 hares, boned (as per illustration)

CABBAGE & MUSHROOM GARNISH
50 g garlic butter
olive oil
50 g shallots, chopped
400 g oriental mushrooms, sliced
½ Chinese cabbage, finely sliced

To make pommes dauphin, grate potatoes on mandoline or coarse grater. Do not wash. Season potatoes with salt and pepper. Heat a little butter in a blini pan and add enough shredded potato to fill the pan. Gently fry until golden brown and then turn over, continue cooking until potatoes are cooked through. Turn out and keep aside until needed. These may be reheated in a hot oven at the last minute. To prepare the mushroom sauce, add chopped shallots to a stainless steel pan with port and Madeira, add dried mushrooms and place on heat.

Bring to the boil and reduce by half, add hare jus and continue to simmer for 10 minutes then add cream. Reduce heat and infuse sauce for 30 minutes. Remove from heat and sieve, pressing out all the juices from the mushrooms. Season. Keep warm until needed or cool until needed and reheat by quickly bringing to the boil. If reheating, pass through a sieve again and correct seasoning. To prepare the crown roast, heat a little oil in a black iron pan and season and seal crown roast of hare. Cook in a very hot oven for 5-10 minutes. Remove from oven and rest for 5 minutes before serving. Brush with butter before resting. To prepare the cabbage and mushroom garnish, heat a little butter and olive oil in a wok or frying pan, add chopped shallots and mushrooms, season and sauté until browned. Remove from wok and add a little more butter and oil, add cabbage and quickly stir-fry until wilted. Add mushrooms back to pan and toss quickly, correct seasoning. To assemble, place a ring or cutter on plate and fill with cabbage mixture. Remove ring. Place pommes dauphin on top and crown roast of hare on top of that. Pour the sauce over and garnish with a few sprigs of chervil or chopped chives. The hare may be served in a variety of ways when cooked this way. Another favourite is with saffron pasta and wood mushrooms together with the cepe cream or with a jus. A good Shiraz or Cabernet blend is best drunk with hare. Serves 4.

FORTY ONE RESTAURANT, SYDNEY, NEW SOUTH WALES.

SALAD OF ROAST DUCK, SEA SCALLOPS & SICHUAN PICKLED CUCUMBERS

SICHUAN PICKLED CUCUMBERS

8 continental cucumbers

3 tablespoons sea salt

1 cup peanut oil

10 small dried chillies

2 large knobs ginger, julienned

8 long red chillies, seeded and julienned

20 dried black shiitake mushrooms, soaked, rinsed well and sliced

½ cup rice wine vinegar

½ cup yellow rock sugar

1 tablespoon Sichuan peppercorns, roasted and ground

SCALLOPS

peanut oil

18 large sea scallops

DRESSING

1 cup juices from the cavity of the duck

3 tablespoons hoisin sauce

20 rocket leaves

6 wing beans, blanched and sliced

1 duck, roasted, plus reserved juices

To make the Sichuan pickled cucumbers, cut the ends off the cucumbers and halve. Scrape out the seeds and cut each half into 4 cm blocks, then into batons. Place in a bowl, sprinkle with salt, and leave to stand for an hour. Squeeze the water out of the cucumbers and pat dry with a paper towel. Heat the oil in a wok and add the dried chillies. Once they blacken, remove from the heat. Add the ginger, chillies, shiitake mushrooms, vinegar, sugar and ground Sichuan peppercorns.

STATE OF ABUNDANCE

Diversity and abundance are the words that spring to mind when considering the epicurean delights of Sydney. Our featured dishes — including Confit of Greenlip Abalone with Black Fungi, Noodle Salad & Truffle Oil Dressing; Goats' Cheese Ravioli with Persillade Sauce; Korean-style Tuna Tartare; and Grilled Marinated Quail on Hummus & Chick Pea Salad with Paprika Oil — offer a tempting glimpse of the culinary pleasures that await you in this city of foodlovers.

Sydney's eating scene is vast and varied and a serious challenge to even the most dedicated gourmet. You'll find it difficult to know where to start — Darlinghurst, Double Bay, Chinatown, Newtown, Leichhardt, Oxford Street, Bondi, The Rocks, Paddington, Surrey Hills, Glebe, Rose Bay and Manly. All boast an excellent range of eateries.

Given such a vast choice, you could easily get the impression that if you can't find your favourite cuisine in Sydney, you won't find it anywhere.

Stir well. Add the cucumber. Stir to incorporate, then place in a sterilised jar. To prepare the scallops, heat some oil in a frypan until smoking and sear the scallops in batches. It is very important that the scallops seal properly and don't stew. They should have a firm crust but still be rare inside. Rest them in a warm place. To make the dressing, place the juices from the cavity of the duck and the hoisin sauce in a small saucepan. Stir to mix, and reduce by half. Allow to cool slightly. Put the rocket and wing beans in a bowl and toss with some of the dressing. Slice the meat off the duck breast and legs, leaving it in large diamonds of about 2 cm square. To serve, place the pickled cucumbers on the base of each plate. Place the wing beans and rocket on top of the cucumber. Place 2 pieces of duck on top of the mound then place 3 scallops around the outside. Pour the remaining dressing over the scallops, and serve. There should be lots of dressing, and it's great mopped up with good sourdough bread. Serves 6.

ROCKPOOL, SYDNEY, NEW SOUTH WALES.

Above: The Rocks, one of Sydney's most historic areas and a tourist mecca.

The monorail carries travellers from the city
centre to Darling Harbour, Sydney's most
ambitious city development to date. Covering
54 hectares, this major tourist attraction
includes a shopping and
restaurant complex, a Convention and
Exhibition Centre, the Australian National
Maritime Museum, the IMAX Movie
Theatre, the Sydney Aquarium, the
Powerhouse Museum, the Chinese Garden of
Friendship and the Sydney Harbour Casino.

CARAMELISED LEMON
SANDWICH

6 sheets fillo pastry
50 g butter, melted
1 lemon
1 ½ cups lemon filling
TOFFEE
1 cup hot water
1 cup sugar

Pre-heat the oven to 180°C. Place a sheet of fillo on a flat surface and brush with melted butter. Top with another sheet. Make three or four circles about 10 cm in diameter. Place each circle on a greased baking tray. Repeat with remaining fillo making 12 double circles in total. Bake for about 8 minutes until golden and crisp. Cool on a wire rack. Thinly peel the lemon and cut peel in julienne slices. Blanch in boiling water for 2 minutes then drain and pat dry. Prepare the toffee by boiling the water and sugar in a saucepan or in the microwave on high power for about 20 minutes until golden. Stir twice during cooking. Toss the lemon peel in a little of the toffee. To assemble, place six cooked pastry rounds on a flat surface. Spread with lemon filling, top with remaining pastry rounds. Garnish with caramelised lemon peel and drizzle with a little extra toffee. Serve on individual plates with a little strawberry purée.
Serves 6.

AREA, SYDNEY, NEW SOUTH
WALES.

LEMON FILLING

½ cup each cornflour, sugar
¾ cup water
¼ cup lemon juice
75 g butter
3 egg yolks
grated rind 1 lemon

To make the filling, combine the cornflour, sugar, water, lemon juice and butter in a saucepan and cook over simmering water, stirring until thick. Cool. Beat in the yolks and grated lemon rind.

La Mensa's Jerusalem Artichoke Soup

250 g each Jerusalem artichokes, potatoes
1 large onion, diced
1 clove garlic, crushed
½ stalk celery
1 bay leaf
125 g butter
1 litre milk
salt and pepper
pinch ground nutmeg
6 tablespoons cream

Peel and cut up the artichokes and potatoes. Place with the onion, garlic, celery and bay leaf in a large saucepan with half of the butter. Cover tightly and stew over low heat for 10 minutes, giving the pan an occasional stir. Pour in the milk and leave to simmer until the vegetables are soft. Purée the vegetables adding more milk if needed to adjust the consistency. Correct the seasoning. Finally stir in the last of the butter and the cream. The top can be sprinkled with chopped parsley and chives.
Serves 4-6.

La Mensa, Sydney, New
South Wales.

Left & Inset: The remarkable Queen Victoria Building, which monopolizes an entire city block. Built during the 1890s' depression as Sydney's main market, it was lovingly restored in the 1980s.

KOREAN-STYLE TUNA TARTARE

2 medium carrots
4 spring onions
400 g piece fresh yellowfin tuna
1 small Chinese cabbage heart, finely shredded
leaves from 1 bunch coriander
3 tablespoons roasted pine nuts
2 quantities sesame dressing
4 raw egg yolks
2 tablespoons sesame seeds, toasted
freshly ground white pepper

Cut the carrots and spring onions into a fine julienne and soak in ice-water for half an hour. Place the tuna on a chopping board, and remove the skin. Cut into 5 mm thick rounds, then cut it lengthwise into 5 mm strips. Place the tuna, carrots, spring onions, cabbage, coriander, pine nuts and dressing in a bowl. Toss to dress and divide between 4 plates. Make a little well in the centre of each, and place an egg yolk on top. Sprinkle with sesame seeds and pepper. Serve immediately. Serves 4.

ROCKPOOL, SYDNEY, NEW SOUTH WALES.

Pages 28-29: The Three Sisters, the most famous landmark in the Blue Mountains. Rising from the coastal plain just 65 kilometres west of Sydney, the Blue Mountains are justly famous for their spectacular scenery.

SWORDFISH STEAK WITH KERALA CURRY

KERALA CURRY

1 teaspoon mustard seeds

2 tablespoons oil for frying

4 each red and green chillies, seeded and finely chopped

250 g finely diced onions

100 g each puréed garlic, puréed ginger

2 teaspoons each red chilli powder, turmeric powder

3¼ cups tomato concasse

150 g fresh coconut, peeled and grated

4 whole curry leaves

SWORDFISH

1 swordfish steak

ghee for cooking

GARNISH

150 g grated coconut, toasted

4 cloves garlic, thinly sliced and fried

4 large red chillies, sliced and fried

1 bunch basil leaves, fried

To make the curry, roast the mustard seeds in the oil, add the chillies and sauté for 2 minutes. Mix the onions with the garlic and ginger purée and add to the pot. After 10 minutes add the spices, tomato concasse, coconut and curry leaves. Cook the curry slowly for 3 hours, adding water or fish stock when it looks dry. Season with salt and pepper. (The curry can be prepared the day before.) Pan-fry swordfish steak in ghee. Add about 1 cup curry when one side is cooked and simmer until cooked. Prepare garnish by mixing all the ingredients together. Sprinkle on swordfish. Can be accompanied with rice. Curry makes 1 litre, enough for 4-6 steaks.

BAYSWATER BRASSERIE, SYDNEY, NEW SOUTH WALES.

The Hunter Valley, a two-hour drive north
of Sydney, is home to some 70 wineries.
These range in size from the big international
names to small boutique operations offering
distinctive, limited-edition wines.

The Hunter Valley is Australia's oldest
commercial wine-producing area, with the
first vintages dating from the 1830s. The
Hunter's table wines, both white and red, still
rank among the best in Australia.

GOATS' CHEESE RAVIOLI WITH PERSILLADE SAUCE

GOATS' CHEESE RAVIOLI FILLING

500 g ricotta cheese
375 g mild goats' cheese
zest of ½ lemon
½ cup each garlic oil, grated pecorino cheese
salt and pepper
nutmeg
cayenne pepper

Combine all ingredients.

PERSILLADE SAUCE FOR RAVIOLI

4 cups parsley sprigs
2 cups basil leaves
125 g gherkins
¼ brown onion
1 clove garlic
125 g roasted and peeled green capsicum
375 ml extra virgin oil
salt and pepper

Combine all ingredients in blender.
Purée until smooth.

PASTA DOUGH

1¾ cups flour
2 eggs
¼ teaspoon each salt, white pepper

basil leaves
parmesan cheese

In a mixer, add eggs to the flour, mixing continuously then season with salt and pepper. Note: Consistency can be adjusted by adding cold water, a few drops at a time. Roll out pasta dough in pasta machine to about 2 mm. Lay out in square moulds. Fill and seal with another layer of rolled-out pasta. (These should be placed in the freezer overnight as they will be much easier to handle.) To serve, drop the ravioli in boiling salted water until they float to the top and are tender to the bite, about 5 minutes. Toss ravioli in a bowl with the persillade sauce. Garnish with deep-fried basil leaves and Parmesan shavings.

Serves 4.

BAYSWATER BRASSERIE, SYDNEY, NEW SOUTH WALES.

Above: Australia's most powerful lighthouse is situated on the continent's most easterly point at Cape Byron. The area is also renowned for its surf. Boardriders gravitate from near and far to Wategos Beach on Cape Byron.

BAKED FIGS WITH GORGONZOLA SAUCE

4 slices prosciutto
4 fresh figs
½ tablespoon butter
1 cup cream
50 g Gorgonzola cheese

Pre-heat oven to 190°C. Wrap one slice of prosciutto around the middle of each fig and secure with a toothpick. Melt butter, cream and Gorgonzola in a saucepan on a low heat. Place figs in an ovenproof dish, pour sauce over and cover with foil. Bake for 7 minutes. Remove foil and bake for a further minute. To serve, place two figs on each plate and pour over sauce. Add fresh pepper to taste. Serves 2.

BUON RICORDO RESTAURANT, SYDNEY, NEW SOUTH WALES.

GRILLED MARINATED QUAIL ON HUMMUS & CHICK PEA SALAD WITH PAPRIKA OIL

PAPRIKA OIL

2 cups olive oil

3 tablespoons sweet paprika

QUAIL SPICE MIX

2 tablespoons each ground cumin, crushed coriander

2 teaspoons each sweet paprika, crushed black peppercorns

HUMMUS

500 g chick peas

1 onion

½ cup tahini (sesame paste)

4 cloves garlic, crushed

salt

½ cup lemon juice

½ teaspoon cumin

QUAIL

3 quail breasts (or 1 single boned, butterflied quail) per serve

olive oil to cover

lemon juice

chick peas, cooked, kept in a little oil

pine nuts, toasted

coriander leaves

sweet paprika

HERB SALAD

chives, parsley leaves, tarragon, dill, chervil, mint, curly endive

vinaigrette

To make paprika oil, place paprika in pan and whisk in oil to mix well. Heat carefully to 140°C, remove and leave to cool. Strain through a fine sieve twice and keep in a squeeze bottle for service. To make quail spice mix, blend all ingredients well and keep in an air-tight container.
To make hummus, soak the chick peas overnight, drain, and rinse well.

Cover well with fresh water and add the onion. Bring to a simmer and cook until very soft. Drain over a pot, reserving 1 cup of the cooking liquid, and discard the onion. Stir the tahini to blend in its oil. Place tahini in a food processor with garlic, salt and lemon juice and blend until the mixture whitens. With machine running add the reserved cooking liquid and the chick peas and process until the mixture is well blended. Remove and push through a wire sieve with the aid of a wooden 'mushroom'. Correct seasoning with salt, cumin and lemon juice. Keep in air-tight containers in fridge until needed. Serve at room temperature. To prepare quail, remove bones and sprinkle with spice mix. Place in a container with olive oil and marinate well. (The oil preserves the quails and keeps them longer as well as marinating them.) Remove from the oil and leave to drain. Grill quail on a flat-top grill, keeping it moist. Remove from grill and sprinkle with a little lemon juice. Meanwhile, spread some hummus onto the centre of plate and form a well in the centre. Sprinkle hummus with some cooked chick peas, pine nuts, coriander leaves, paprika, paprika oil and lemon juice. Top with cooked quail. Toss herb salad with vinaigrette, place near quail and serve.
Serves 1.

CICADA, POTTS POINT,
NEW SOUTH WALES.

Left: Warrumbungle National Park, 490 kilometres north-west of Sydney, has some of the nation's most spectacular scenery.

SALAD OF BEETROOT, ASPARAGUS, MACHE & GOATS' CHEESE

VINAIGRETTE

100 ml each walnut oil, olive oil
50 ml red wine vinegar
salt and pepper

SALAD

10 asparagus spears, peeled
1 beetroot, boiled, skinned, cut into
small wedges
mache (lamb's lettuce)
curly endive
1 tablespoon pine nuts, toasted
100 g fresh goats' cheese
chopped chives
chervil sprigs

To prepare the vinaigrette, mix walnut oil, olive oil and red wine vinegar with salt and pepper to taste. Cook asparagus in boiling salted water for approximately 3 minutes. Remove, drain well, season and toss with a little vinaigrette. Meanwhile, toss beetroot with some vinaigrette and arrange on a plate leaving a space in the centre. Toss mache and curly endive in vinaigrette and place in the centre of the beetroot. Arrange the dressed asparagus on the salads and sprinkle over pine nuts. Slice the fresh goats' cheese and place on the salad, sprinkle with chopped chives and chervil sprigs. Mix a little of the beetroot cooking juices with an equal amount of vinaigrette and spoon around the salad. Serve immediately. Serves 2.

CICADA, POTTS POINT, NEW SOUTH WALES.

Above: The arid desert country of far west New South Wales, surrounding Broken Hill.

Left: The restored ghost town of Silverton, 23 kilometres from Broken Hill, is more than a tourist attraction. It's a familiar movie location, featuring in A Town Like Alice, Razorback and Mad Max II.

SNAPPER WITH CANNELLINI BEANS & TRUFFLE OIL

*2 cups dry cannellini beans (Great
Northern beans)
3 tablespoons fresh
breadcrumbs
1 tablespoon water
2 tablespoons diced tomato
4 leaves basil, shredded
extra virgin olive oil
salt and pepper
2 x 400 g whole snapper
flour for dipping
truffle oil to garnish*

Soak the cannellini beans in cold water
to cover overnight. Bring to the boil in
fresh water to cover and simmer 2-3
hours until tender. In a small bowl mix
together the breadcrumbs, water,
tomato, basil and 1 tablespoon oil.
Season to taste. Fillet the snapper and
dust the skin with flour. Heat 1
tablespoon of olive oil in a frying pan.
When hot, place the snapper skin side
down. Place in oven and bake at
200°C for 4 minutes, turn and cook
for a further 4 minutes. Warm
cannellini beans and season. On a
serving plate, place beans then snapper
on top, skin side up. With a fork
scatter the breadcrumb mixture on top
of the beans. Add a few generous
drops of truffle oil on fish and beans.
Serves 2.

BUON RICORDO RESTAURANT,
SYDNEY, NEW SOUTH WALES.

*A bird's-eye view of a Snowy Mountains ski
field. All the ski resorts are within Kosciusko
National Park. Mount Kosciusko (2228 m)
is the highest point in Australia.*

TARTARE OF YELLOWFIN TUNA WITH BEETROOT OIL & OSCIETRE CAVIAR

200 ml beetroot juice
2 tablespoons Japanese rice vinegar
1 tablespoon canola oil
400 g yellowfin tuna
salt and pepper
juice of 1 lemon
3 teaspoons mayonnaise
1 teaspoon crème fraiche or sour cream
4 quail eggs, soft boiled
4 teaspoons each Oscietre caviar,
salmon roe
4 sprigs chervil
extra virgin olive oil
2 teaspoons chopped chives

Place the beetroot juice in a clean stainless steel pan and put on a high heat until it has reduced by three-quarters. Add the vinegar and reduce to a syrup. Remove from the heat and whisk in the canola oil. Leave to cool. Finely dice the tuna and place in a bowl, season with salt and pepper, add the lemon juice to taste and then add the mayonnaise and crème fraiche. Mix well and taste for seasoning. Do not use too much salt as the caviar is salty and will compensate for this. Place a pastry ring mould on the plate and fill with a quarter of the tuna mix, press down and smooth over the top. Remove the ring and garnish the top with the quail egg cut in half, both types of caviar and the sprig of chervil. Carefully spoon a little of the intense beetroot oil around the plate, drizzle with extra virgin olive oil and sprinkle with chives. Serve with toasted sourdough bread.

Wine suggestion: this dish works well with Champagne, preferably a house style such as Krug, Bollinger or Louis Roederer. Alternatively a Semillon or Chardonnay would work equally well. Serves 4.

FORTY ONE RESTAURANT, SYDNEY, NEW SOUTH WALES.

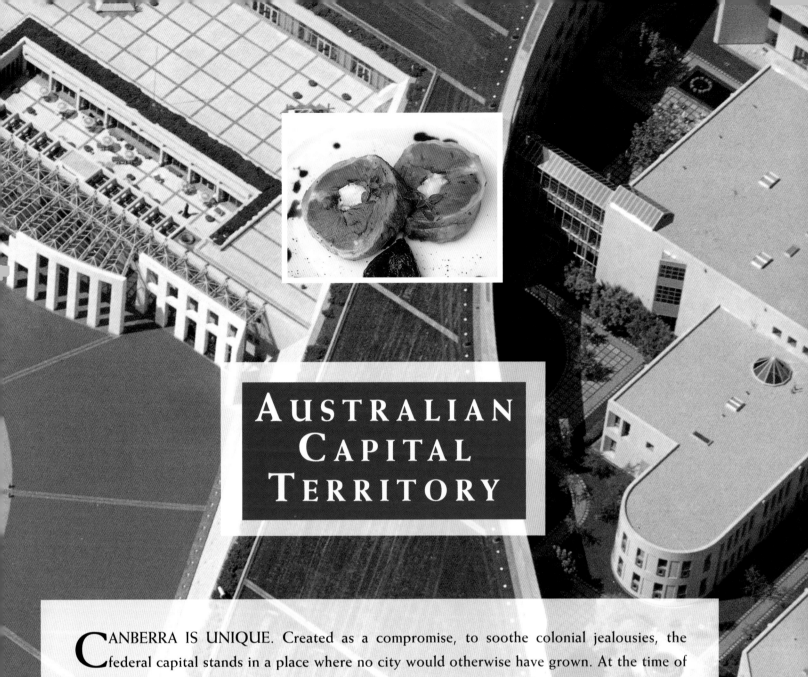

AUSTRALIAN CAPITAL TERRITORY

CANBERRA IS UNIQUE. Created as a compromise, to soothe colonial jealousies, the federal capital stands in a place where no city would otherwise have grown. At the time of federation in 1901, there was intense Sydney-Melbourne rivalry, over which was Australia's chief city. After prolonged wrangling, the Commonwealth government bought land for the Australian Capital Territory — thereafter known as 'the ACT' — and developed one of the world's best-known, fully planned cities.

Here you will find some of the most striking and eclectic architecture in Australia. Completed in 1988, at a cost of $1.2 billion, the new Parliament House (pictured) is, like many other important buildings, and Canberra itself, the result of an architectural competition. You can also view some of the country's best exhibitions here: the world's finest collection of Aboriginal art and an outstanding display of Australian and European works at the National Gallery of Australia. The country's biggest collection of books — over five million — together with rare manuscripts and maps and Captain Cook's *Endeavour* journal can be found at the National Library. And the massive Australian War Memorial is one of Australia's most frequently visited attractions.

A trip to the 'diplomatic belt' at Yarralumla is also worthwhile. Embassies have frequent open days, with displays from their homelands.

ILLABO LAMB WITH MILAWA GOATS' CHEESE & GRILLED FIGS

FARCE

1 small onion, chopped
50 ml olive oil
1 teaspoon each chopped oregano, thyme
½ teaspoon rosemary
1-2 cloves garlic, chopped
1 teaspoon crushed pepper
pinch sea salt
meat trimmings from saddle

1 whole saddle of lamb, deboned with skin intact, meat divided into loin and fillet
300 g Milawa goats' cheese
extra virgin olive oil
6 figs
balsamic vinegar
sprigs oregano

To prepare the farce, sweat the onion in olive oil, add herbs and garlic, pepper and salt. Cool then blend in food processor with the lamb trimmings. To prepare the lamb, stretch out the skin of the lamb and cover evenly with the farce. Lay down one loin from end to end. Roll goats' cheese into a log. Place a log on top of the loin, then place the other loin on top of this. Use the small fillets to fill in the sides so that the goats' cheese is completely covered. Then roll skin around the log tightly until overlapped by about 3 cm. Tie with butchers twine every 2 cm. The lamb may be roasted whole or in individual servings. For single servings heat olive oil in pan and seal all sides before roasting.

Place in 180°-200°C oven for 10-15 minutes until pink. Cut figs in half, oil, and char-grill until soft. Remove meat from oven, set aside for 5 minutes. Remove string then cut portions. Drizzle olive oil on plate, then some balsamic vinegar so that the oil catches the vinegar. Place lamb and figs on plates and garnish with oregano sprigs.
Serves 6.

FRINGE BENEFITS RESTAURANT & WINE BAR, CANBERRA CITY, ACT.

Inset: Parliament House. Eight years in the building, at a cost of $1.2 billion, it opened in 1988 replacing the 'temporary' parliament house which served for 11 years longer than its intended 50-year life.

Left: Canberra — a purpose-built monument to national aspirations. And Australia's largest inland city.

Following page 51: The Captain Cook Memorial jets 130 metres into the air above Lake Burley Griffin, the centrepiece of Canberra.

CHAR-GRILLED QUAIL WITH THAI-STYLE SALAD

2 each shallots, cloves garlic, thinly sliced
oil
2 tablespoons peanuts, chopped

NAM JIM DRESSING
4 small chillies
3 coriander roots
3 garlic cloves
salt
3 shallots
2 tablespoons each palm sugar, fish sauce
(quantity varies according to strength of
other ingredients)
2 cups lime juice

QUAIL
1 jumbo quail per person, boned but with
leg and winglets intact

SALAD
2 coriander sprigs
2 shallots or spring onions, curled
1 slice green paw paw, julienned
4 Vietnamese mint leaves

Place shallots in oil in a frying pan and cook until brown and crisp. Spread on a paper towel. Repeat with the garlic. Fry peanuts until brown and then drain. To prepare dressing, bruise the chilli, coriander root, garlic and salt in a mortar and pestle. Add sliced shallots, palm sugar, fish sauce and lime juice. Let stand. Makes enough for 8 servings. Char-grill quail until pink, leave whole. To assemble, place quail on plate. Toss salad ingredients with some nam jim and place on top of quail, dress with extra nam jim, then sprinkle with fried ingredients.

SERVES 1.

FRINGE BENEFITS RESTAURANT & WINE BAR, CANBERRA CITY, ACT.

CAPITAL CUISINE

Given that the federal capital plays host to the diplomatic corps, it's no surprise to find so many cafés, brasseries and restaurants offering a wide range of ethnic dishes along with local specialities including grain-fed beef, milk-fed lamb and fresh seafood from the nearby New South Wales south coast. The Canberra area also has 17 wineries producing a good range of fine cool climate vintages.

The accent in 'embassy city' is on choice. Around the City Centre you can sample Italian, Thai, Pakistani, Chinese, Malaysian, Lebanese, African and modern Australian cuisine. Dickson's Wooley Street, although largely Asian in flavour, also offers a taste of Russian and Italian cuisine. Upmarket and cosmopolitan, Manuka offers modern Australian cuisine to French, Malaysian, Chinese and award-winning Turkish dishes.

In Canberra, you don't have to be a diplomat to dine like one.

VICTORIA

FOR AUSTRALIA'S SMALLEST mainland state, Victoria packs in a wealth of attractions. From the glittering lights of Melbourne (pictured) to the grand isolation of the Snowy River wilderness, from the sunny Murray Valley wine country to the historic goldfields regions of Ballarat and Bendigo to one of the world's great drives along the wild southern coast, Victoria will surprise you with its unsurpassed diversity.

Australia's second biggest tourist attraction — the evening parade of the fairy penguins on Phillip Island — lies within easy driving distance of Melbourne. Afterwards try the famous lobster dinner. Seafood afficionados should follow the coast north to the centre of 'Victoria's Riviera', Lakes Entrance, a thriving tourist centre and the home port for Australia's largest fishing fleet. Much of the succulent seafood taken from these waters — snapper, tuna, salmon, bream and prawns — tempts the palates of Melbourne diners. The Gippsland area also boasts the 'Gourmet Deli Trail'. Follow your appetite north-west to the 'Milawa Gourmet Country' and on through Ned Kelly territory to the palate-pleasing delights of the oldest wine-growing district in Australia, centred on Rutherglen.

Whether cruising the mighty Murray River by paddle-steamer and feasting on yabbies as the sun sets on Australia's greatest inland waterway or gorging yourself on the gourmet delights and the spectacular scenery along the Great Ocean Road on the 'Cappuccino Coast', you will find Victoria is Australia at its most civilized.

ORANGE PARFAIT WITH ALMOND TUILLE

6 egg yolks
200 g castor sugar
150 ml water
3 tablespoons orange liqueur
600 ml whipping cream, beaten until thick
zest of 1 orange
2 almond tuilles per serving
icing sugar for dusting

Beat egg yolks until thick. Combine sugar and water in saucepan, bring to the boil, stirring to dissolve the sugar. Add liqueur and bring back to the boil. (When surface is evenly bubbling it is ready.) Pour hot syrup in a thin stream over egg yolks while beating. Continue beating until cool, the mixture becomes white and fluffy. Chill mixture. Fold in beaten cream and orange zest. Line a 1.5 litre mould (suitable for freezing) with plastic film. Add the parfait mixture. Cover and freeze. To serve, unmould the parfait, cut in slices, place on plate and layer between two almond tuilles. Dust with icing sugar. Garnish as desired.

Serves 6-8.

ISIS, MELBOURNE, VICTORIA.

MOST LIVABLE CITY

Melbourne is Australia's most stylish city. Architecturally a striking blend of past and present — and home to more than three million people — the country's second-largest metropolis lays claim to being the fashion, food and cultural capital of Australia. Here you will find the good life is a way of life.

With thousands of restaurants, cafés, delis, bistros and brasseries Melbourne is a wonderful place to indulge your appetite. Our featured dishes — including Peking Duck, Antipasto Del Bàcaro, and Honeyed Quail Baked in an Eggplant — offer an exciting taste of the gastronomic world tour that awaits you. Chinatown is one of the best and most diverse food precincts. Here you can sample superb Chinese cuisines along with the best of Malaysian and Thai dishes. Southgate — one of the city's premiere restaurant belts on the south bank of the Yarra River — offers

you a great range of styles and prices. Carlton has Lygon Street, Melbourne's Italian centre, famous for inexpensive, giant-size servings of pasta and pizza and quality cappuccino and gelati. In Richmond you'll find Swan Street, the Greek heartland. Here, the Mediterranean delights include spit-roasted lamb, char-grilled octopus, fetta cheese and Taramasalata. If you fancy Vietnamese food, Victoria Street — 'Little Saigon' — lined with dozens of bargain-priced restaurants, is a must. St Kilda is Melbourne's most famous beachside suburb. The Esplanade is a favourite for alfresco dining, offering a range of styles from mediterranean through to modern Australian cuisine. Acland Street, which the Jewish community has made its own, is renowned for its cafés and cake shops. Not a place for the calorie-conscious! Fitzroy boasts Brunswick Street, the ultimate in sheer variety — Indian, Thai, Turkish, French, Malaysian, Ethiopian, Greek, Indonesian, Japanese, Afghani, South American and modern Australian.

Not surprisingly, an international survey has acclaimed Melbourne as the most livable city in the world.

Melbourne's suburbs sprawl round Port Phillip Bay — viewed from Brighton Beach. The city centre is sited on the Yarra River, about 5 kilometres inland from the bay.

ANTIPASTO DEL BÀCARO

Frittata slice
Crostino (ricotta & basil pesto)
Grissino
Zucca al forno con rosmarino (oven-
baked pumpkin with rosemary)
Melanzane alla griglia con olio díoliva,
aglio & prezzemolo (char-grilled eggplant
with olive oil, parsley & garlic)
Salami
Zucchine marinati con aceto bianco
(zucchini marinated in white vinegar)
Funghi saltati allíaglio, olio e
prezzemolo (mushrooms sautéed in olive
oil, garlic & parsley)
Prosciutto
Peperoni grigliati allíolio, aglio &
basilico (grilled capsicums with olive oil,
garlic & basil)
Sardina marinata allíolio e limone
(sardines marinated in olive oil & lemon)

IL BÀCARO, MELBOURNE,
VICTORIA.

Below: The Melbourne Cup — the horserace that brings the nation to a standstill on the first Tuesday in November.

PEKING DUCK

1 young plump duck, approximately
2 kg, meticulously cleaned

FILLING

1 teaspoon Chinese Five Spice powder
1 knob of ginger (size of thumb)
1 clove garlic
1½ tablespoons Chinese rice wine
(Shaohsing) or dry sherry
¼ teaspoon salt
1 teaspoon sugar
2 or 3 stalks spring onions, trimmed

BASTING MIXTURE

2-3 tablespoons each Chinese maltose,
white vinegar
2 tablespoons Chinese rice wine
(Shaohsing) or dry sherry

Place filling ingredients inside cavity of duck and close opening carefully with a skewer or using a needle and thread. Pull skin over top of neck opening, and knot some string around to close opening neck. Tie a loose, loop knot around the neck leaving enough string to hang up the duck. Insert a pump between the skin and meat at the neck opening and pump in enough air to puff up the duck. Immediately pull the loop knot to tighten it, which traps the air inside the duck. The duck is blown up like a balloon. Hang up on a hook. Bring a wok full of water to rolling boil, and immerse the duck (holding by the neck) into the boiling water for a brief moment. The skin instantly contracts, shrinking to give a tight, smooth skin. Heat the basting ingredients and baste the duck thoroughly with this mixture by pouring over the entire skin. Repeat a few times.

The basting mixture should be warm/hot. Hang to dry overnight. To roast, pre-heat oven to 190°C for 10 minutes, then place duck on an open rack in the centre of the oven. Place a pan with a small amount of water at the bottom of the oven to catch any drips. Roast breast side up for 25 minutes, then carefully turn over and roast breast side down for 20 minutes. The skin should roast to a crisp golden brown.
Serves 8.

FLOWER DRUM, MELBOURNE, VICTORIA.

Left: Standing tall on the Yarra River. One of the city's great strengths is its multiculturalism (it's the world's second-largest Greek city), with people from dozens of ethnic backgrounds from over 140 countries.

Below: Symbol of a city — the tram. There is even a tram restaurant that cruises the streets of Melbourne every night.

BARBECUED OX-TONGUE WITH TASMANIAN GOLD POTATOES, SNAKE BEANS & STICKY MUSTARD SEED DRESSING

4 pickled ox tongues

2 kg mirepoix, chopped

2 teaspoons salt

¼ cup white vinegar

DRESSING

2 cups white wine vinegar

1¼ cups Champagne vinegar

¾ cup water

3¼ cups white sugar

4 tablespoons yellow mustard seeds, soaked

3 tablespoons grain mustard

1 kg Tasmanian Southern Gold potatoes

500 g snake beans

Simmer tongues in water with mirepoix, salt and vinegar for approximately 4 hours or until soft to touch. Let cool in stock. Peel tongues and remove excess fat and tissue. Refrigerate tongues in stock. Once chilled, slice tongues lengthways on a meat slicer. Cover with damp cloth, plastic film and refrigerate. To make dressing, place vinegars, water and sugar in a saucepan and reduce by between one third to one half. Once reduction is sticky, add yellow mustard seeds and grain mustard. Store at room temperature. Note: This dressing has to be completely cool to gauge the correct consistency. To garnish, steam and peel Southern Gold potatoes.

Blanch snake beans and chop finely. To serve, sauté potatoes and snake beans and place in the centre of a deep, flat bowl. Chargrill tongue and place in 'rolls' on top of the potatoes and beans. Dress with sticky mustard seed dressing. Serves about 8.

GUERNICA RESTAURANT, FITZROY, VICTORIA.

Left and below: Queen Victoria Gardens. Melbourne has 680 hectares of magnificent landscaped parks and gardens. The city's supreme park, regarded as one of the world's finest, is the Royal Botanic Gardens.

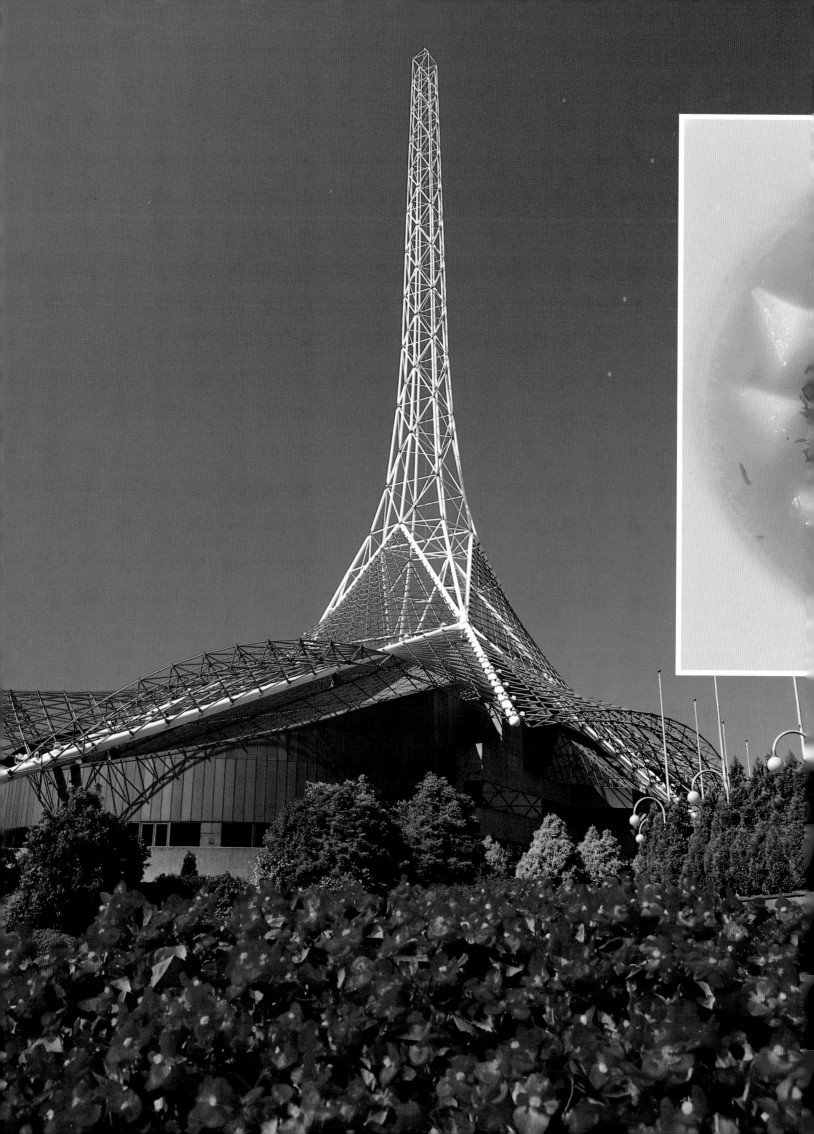

Arts Mecca

Melbourne likes to think of itself as the arts capital of Australia. And with good reason. In addition to the opulent Victorian Arts Centre and the National Gallery of Victoria, which houses world-class collections of Australian, Aboriginal, Asian, European and Pre-Columbian art, the city boasts over one hundred independent galleries along with a myriad of museums devoted to everything from the performing arts, architecture, natural history, science and technology through to sport. Theatre is unsurpassed, offering everything from smash-hit musicals to classic and contemporary drama to experimental works at the legendary La Mama. Widely acknowledged as the country's rock capital, Melbourne's pub music circuit has produced some of Australia's most famous bands. The International Festival of the Arts is world-class.

SCAROLA

This is a very simply prepared soup with lots of flavour.

200 ml olive oil
1 large onion, finely diced
4 cloves garlic, sliced
3 large pontiac potatoes
1 bunch curly endive
1.5-1.8 litres chicken stock
salt and pepper

In a 5 litre saucepan heat 150 ml olive oil. Add onion, garlic and the potatoes peeled and diced in 1 cm cubes. Sauté this for 3-4 minutes. Season ingredients a little at this stage. Add curly endive, outer leaves removed, base removed, cut in half and well washed. Sauté another 1-2 minutes. Make sure ingredients don't stick to saucepan. If too dry, add a little more oil. Add chicken stock and bring to a simmer. Cook for 10-15 minutes. Season again to taste. Drizzle with a little good olive oil once in bowl.
Serves 6.

MARCHETTI'S LATIN RESTAURANT, MELBOURNE, VICTORIA.

Left: Victorian Arts Centre. Situated on the banks of the Yarra River, this sumptuous complex is the focal point of Melbourne's social and cultural scene.

WARM SALAD OF SMOKED EEL & SOUTHERN GOLDS

1½ smoked eels
200 g curly endive
8 medium Southern Gold potatoes
sea salt
½ red onion, peeled
½ bunch chives
1 teaspoon Dijon mustard
2 teaspoons white wine vinegar
2 tablespoons extra virgin olive oil
freshly ground white pepper
12 slices very thin streaky bacon

Pre-heat oven to 200°C. Cut heads and tails off eels, peel and cut into four sections. Remove flesh from bone to give 16 pieces – you will need 12. Pick, wash and drain endive. Wash Southern Golds and cook in boiling salted water until just tender. Drain and leave warm. To make the vinaigrette, finely chop the onion, blanch in boiling water for 10 seconds and drain. Finely chop chives. In a bowl whisk together mustard, vinegar and oil. Add onion, chives and seasoning. Lay bacon on a tray and bake in oven until crispy. Drain on a kitchen towel. To serve, lay eel on a tray and warm in oven for 3 minutes. Slice Southern Golds and place in a circle in the centre of four warm plates. Drizzle with some of the vinaigrette. Place three pieces of eel on top of the potatoes. Toss endive with some of the vinaigrette and place on top of eel. Place three pieces of bacon on top of endive and serve immediately.
Serves 4.

ADELPHI HOTEL, MELBOURNE, VICTORIA.

VINTAGE VICTORIA

Victoria is a vibrant wine state with over 300 commercial vineyards and 100 smaller operations. No matter where you travel, you will never be far from a tempting vintage. Close to Melbourne — in fact almost in its outer north-eastern suburbs — is the Yarra Valley, eminently suited to producing high-quality reds and whites. The gold country of central Victoria, centred on an axis between Ballarat and Bendigo, offers some excellent wines, mainly reds but some whites and sparkling wines. The scenic Goulbourn Valley is home to historic vineyards producing unusually long-lived reds and quality whites. South and west is the region that produces, along with Great Western sparkling, reds and whites that are well worth seeking out. Head north-west into the Murray Valley border country and you will find yourself in the oldest wine-growing district in Australia, centred on Rutherglen. The region is famed for its rich, flavoursome reds and exotic range of fortified wines. But the sheer diversity of wineries and wines makes this a wine-buff's mecca.

Above: Yarra River vineyards. High-quality Cabernet, Pinot Noir and Chardonnay wines are a specialty.

Left: Sampling a vintage at Seppelts' winery in the Great Western district, an area famous for the sparkling wine of that name.

HONEYED QUAIL BAKED IN AN EGGPLANT

**Served with whipped Bulgarian fetta
cheese**

6 x 180-200 g quail
QUAIL JUS
quail bones
1 each celery stick, onion, carrot, diced
½ cup sweet sherry
2 litres water
2 sprigs thyme
4 juniper berries
EGGPLANT
6 small eggplants (12 cm long)
olive oil
HONEY GLAZE
¼ cup sweet sherry
¼ cup mild honey
2 cardamom pods, cracked
2 teaspoons orange blossom water

200 g Bulgarian fetta
*200 g yoghurt (strained overnight in
cheesecloth)*
2-3 tablespoons Dijon mustard
fresh pepper
watercress to garnish

**Remove neck and wings from quail
leaving the first wing joint attached to
the body. With a sharp knife, cut
through quail backbone opening up
both sides with your hands. Pull out
breast plate and ribs gently and with
a small knife remove wishbones and
all connecting bones. Remove both
thigh bones but leave drumsticks
intact. Re-shape quail back to
original form. Tie drumsticks
together crossing the knuckle and
tie around the breast and
first wing joints.**

To make quail jus, roast quail bones with celery, onion and carrot, adding sweet sherry and topping up pan with the water. Bring to boil and simmer for 3 hours with thyme and juniper berries. Strain and slowly reduce to 200 ml, skimming the top constantly. To prepare the eggplants, use a potato peeler and peel strips the length of the eggplant to achieve a striped effect. Leave the green cap (stem) intact and cut lengthways through the centre of the eggplant until 1 cm from the cap. Sprinkle with salt both around and in the cut. Rest for 2-3 hours in a colander. Rinse completely and roast slowly in an oven at 170°C for 15-20 minutes with a good sprinkling of olive oil. Remove and cool down. To make the glaze, bring sherry to the boil with honey, cardamom and orange blossom water. Cool. In a food processor beat at high speed the fetta cheese with strained yoghurt and mustard. Season with fresh pepper. Refrigerate for 1 hour. Colour quail in a hot pan with olive oil and seasoning (salt and pepper). Brush some honey glaze over the quail and roll the quail in the pan to ensure they are well coated. Remove from heat and cool down. Remove string from quail and place leg end first into the eggplant centre. Tie legs around stem and cook at 200°C in a butter-greased pan for 10 minutes. Remove and rest for 2 minutes. Heat the jus. Place quail on one side of plate and spoon fetta sauce on the other side. Pour hot jus on top of quail and garnish with watercress.

Serves 6.

O'CONNELL'S,
SOUTH MELBOURNE, VICTORIA.

TURKISH COFFEE ICE CREAM WITH HAZELNUT FLORENTINES & FRESH BERRIES

ICE CREAM

200 g castor sugar

½ cup water

100 g liquid glucose

3 cardamom pods, cracked

¼ cup Turkish coffee

60 g chocolate

12 egg yolks

¼ cup Tia Maria

1 litre thickened cream

BERRIES

1 punnet each strawberries, blackberries, raspberries, blueberries

HAZELNUT FLORENTINES

50 g butter

½ cup each pure cream, castor sugar

230 g hazelnuts, toasted, peeled and chopped

100 g crystallised orange peel

½ cup plain flour

chocolate to coat

To make the ice cream, bring to the boil the castor sugar, water, glucose, cardamom, Turkish coffee and chocolate. Simmer for 5 minutes. Whip egg yolks at high speed until light and fluffy. Strain coffee mixture into egg yolks and beat for 1 minute. Add Tia Maria and cream. Refrigerate for 1-2 hours then churn in an ice-cream machine. To prepare the Florentines, bring butter, cream and sugar to the boil. Remove from heat and stir in hazelnuts, orange peel and flour.

ADVENTURE PLAYGROUNDS

Victoria boasts over one hundred national, state, wilderness and regional parks, ranging from desert mallee to rainforests, coasts, volcanic plains and alps. Mount Buffalo National Park (pictured) is popular with bushwalkers in summer and fall. Winter snows provide excellent cross-country skiing. Also in the north-east is the magnificent Alpine National Park, the state's largest

and home to the major ski resorts. In the summer months the area is ideal for rock climbing, bushwalking, canoeing, rafting, hang-gliding, mountain-biking, horse trekking and paragliding. In the scorching environment of the north-west the tremendous variety of wildlife in the Murray-Sunset and Hattah-Kulkyne National Parks has evolved strategies for avoiding or tolerating the oppressive heat and dryness: some burrow, some just rest during the day and some birds ride thermals to cooler air. Just 35 kilometres from Melbourne is the lush green wonderland of the Dandenong Ranges National Park, home to over 20 species of native animals including platypuses, echidnas and sugar gliders. Bird species number over 100. Be prepared to share your picnic spot with kookaburras, rosellas and cockatoos. The most popular national park in Victoria is Wilsons Promontory, a huge granite peninsula that is the southernmost tip of the Australian mainland. Birds and other wildlife abound on 'the Prom'. Emus feed unperturbed. Kangaroos and wallabies seem unimpressed by their human observers. And whether you want surfing, safe swimming or a secluded beach all to yourself, you will find it on 'the Prom'.

Place tablespoonfuls onto silicon paper and flatten with wet fingertips. Bake at 160°C for 8 minutes. Turn tray around and bake for another 8 minutes. Cool Florentines on a cake rack. When cold spread the bases with melted chocolate. To assemble each serving, place a serving of berries in a heap on one side of a chilled plate. Place 2 scoops of ice cream next to the berries. To complete the triangle, place Florentines next to the berries, one chocolate side face up, the other chocolate side face down.
Serves 10.

O'CONNELL'S, SOUTH MELBOURNE, VICTORIA.

PALM SUGAR CARAMELISED RICE PUDDING WITH TOASTED COCONUT ICE CREAM & LIME SYRUP

RICE PUDDING

6 cups coconut milk

2 vanilla beans, scraped

8 egg yolks

¾ cup sugar

1¼ cups short-grain rice

180 g butter, softened

TOASTED COCONUT ICE CREAM

400 g long-thread coconut

1 litre each milk, cream

¼ cup Malibu liqueur

2 cups sugar

24 egg yolks

LIME SYRUP

500 ml water

500 g sugar

juice and zest of 10 limes, separated

500 g palm sugar, finely grated

GARNISH

icing sugar

mint sprigs

To prepare the pudding, bring milk to boil with vanilla beans. Beat egg yolks and sugar until creamy. Add rice to milk and simmer slowly, continuously stirring with a wooden spoon. Once absorbed and of a 'porridge' consistency, beat in the yolks and sugar and continue to cook for a further 5-8 minutes. Then add softened butter, and beat gently until incorporated. You will need 14, 12 cm round by 3 cm high ring moulds. Place rings on parchment paper and lightly spray with non-stick cooking spray.

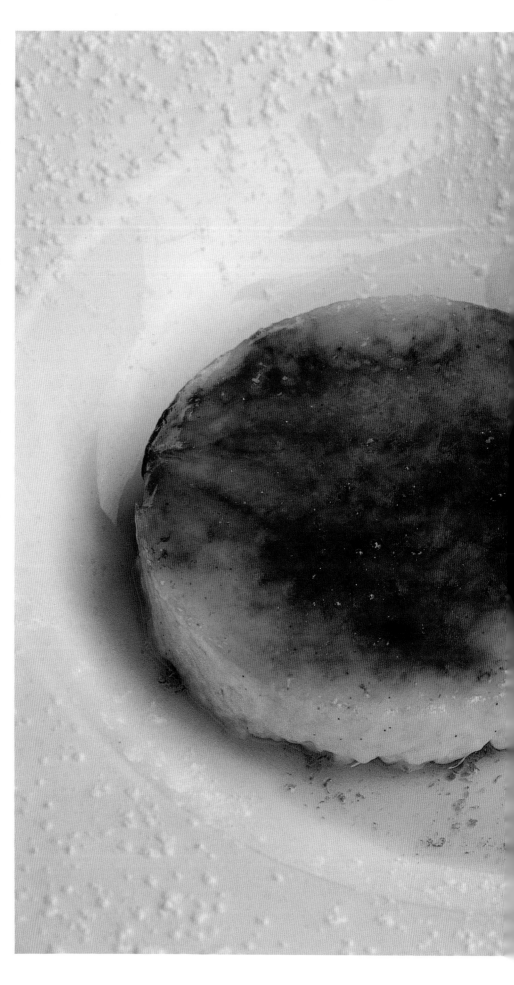

Spoon rice mixture into the moulds and smooth them out with the back of a kitchen spoon. Refrigerate to set. To make ice cream, toast threaded coconut in a hot oven. Add coconut to milk and cream and slowly infuse over a low heat. Once flavoured, strain the milk and cream and add Malibu. Cream sugar and egg yolks. Whisk hot milk and cream mixture over yolks and sugar. Cook over a double boiler until coating consistency. Strain and chill over ice. Churn in an ice-cream machine or food processor and freeze. To make lime syrup, boil water and sugar, add lime juice and reduce by half. Finely grate and blanch lime zest and add to the syrup once cool. To serve, while still in its ring, finely cover the top of the rice puddings with finely grated palm sugar and with a blow-torch caramelise the pudding. Remove from ring and lift into a deep flat bowl and serve accompanied with lime syrup and a small scoop of coconut ice cream. Dust with icing sugar and garnish with a sprig of mint.
Serves 14.

GUERNICA RESTAURANT,
FITZROY, VICTORIA.

STINGRAY & GREEN MANGO SALAD WITH CRISPY FISH

CRISPY FISH
1 kg flathead fillets
salt
STINGRAY
2 kg stingray
MANGO SALAD
150 g palm sugar
300 ml rice wine vinegar
14 green mangoes
7 each Birdseye chillies, garlic cloves,
shallots, ripe tomatoes
250 g peanuts, lightly roasted
1 bunch each holy basil, coriander,
Vietnamese hot mint, leaves picked
and washed
fish sauce
lime juice
crispy fried shallots
wild betel leaves

To prepare crispy fish, skin flathead and remove all bones. Salt fish well and place on a wire rack over a baking tray. Roast in a medium oven for 20 minutes until golden and quite dry. Allow to cool. Blend roasted fish until like bread crumbs. Sprinkle fish into a deep-fryer set at 180°C. Push fish together with a spider to form a raft. Fry until golden and crisp. Drain well. To prepare stingray, steam for 15 minutes until flesh flakes easily from cartilage. Keep warm. To make the mango salad, dissolve palm sugar in rice wine vinegar. Peel and grate the green mangoes. In a mortar grind 1 chilli, 1 garlic clove, 1 shallot and 1 tomato to a paste. Add the equivalent of 2 mangoes, 2 tablespoons lightly roasted peanuts, about 6 each of the herb leaves and grind again.

Dress the salad with about 1 tablespoon of the palm sugar/rice wine vinegar syrup, the juice of half a lime, a shot of fish sauce and some crispy fried shallots. The salad should be hot, sweet and sour. To assemble, shred the flesh of the stingray, keeping the pieces large. Mix about 100 g of the fish into the salad. To serve, place a wild betel leaf on a plate, add the salad and top with a scattering of the crispy fish. This salad is best made in small amounts with a mortar and pestle. Collect all ingredients first and proceed two portions at a time (with the amounts recommended in the recipe). Serves about 8.

STELLA, MELBOURNE, VICTORIA (PRINTED COURTESY OF GEOFF LINDSAY, FROM HIS BOOK *CHOW DOWN*, PUBLISHED BY ALLEN & UNWIN 1997).

Sweeping views over the Grampians from the 'Jaws of Death'. Victoria's most imposing national park, the Grampians form the westernmost heights of the Great Dividing Range.

MARINATED SPATCHCOCK, BLACK RICE & CHILLI JAM

CHILLI JAM

1 litre vegetable oil
6 cloves garlic, finely sliced
100 g green ginger, skinned and finely sliced
6 small red chillies, chopped
4 long red chillies, seeded and chopped
2 red onions, peeled and chopped
4 red capsicums, seeded and chopped
400 g ripe red tomatoes, seeded, skinned and chopped
1 1/4 cups castor sugar
1 cup fish sauce

Using a heavy broad-based saucepan, heat oil until smoking, add garlic, ginger, chillies, onions and capsicums. Cook until lightly coloured, stirring occasionally. Add tomatoes, cook until dark, stirring often. Add sugar and caramelise. Add fish sauce. Blend. Store in the refrigerator. Makes about 4 cups.

MARINADE

3 tablespoons sweet soy (ketjap manis)
100 ml Shaohsing wine
knob ginger, crushed
2 cloves garlic, crushed
1¼ tablespoons tamarind paste
¼ cup each palm sugar, peanut oil
2 red chillies, sliced

1 boned spatchcock or chicken breast per serving
¾ cup cooked black rice per serving

Mix marinade ingredients together. Coat poultry in marinade, cover and refrigerate for at least 12 hours. To cook poultry, seal in pan then cook in a moderate oven. To serve, place black rice, poultry and chilli jam as you choose. Garnish with fine julienne of spring onion.
Serves 1.

ISIS, MELBOURNE, VICTORIA.

WARM PLUM GALETTE

PLUM SAUCE

half an 850 g can plums and all juice
1 vanilla bean
1 teaspoon ground cinnamon
peel of ½ an orange
juice of 1 lemon

FRANGIPANE

100 g each butter, castor sugar
2 eggs
100 g ground almonds, sieved
2 tablespoons plain flour

GALETTE

6 x 14 cm round disks of puff pastry
remaining half of plums from the
850 g can

GARNISH

fresh cherries
icing sugar

To make the sauce, reserve 6 plums for the Galette. Combine all other ingredients in a stainless-steel saucepan. Simmer for 5-10 minutes to infuse flavour. Remove vanilla and peel. Purée. To make the frangipane, beat the butter and sugar then add the eggs. Mix in flour and almonds.

To make the Galette, place pastry disk on a greased baking tray. Spread with frangipane. Arrange plums on top. Bake at 200°C for 10 minutes. Serve on plum sauce, garnished with fresh cherries and dusted with icing sugar.

Serves 6.

BRIDPORT ONE-ONE-SIX, ALBERT PARK, VICTORIA.

ROAD TO SURPRISES

No matter how many roads you have driven, the Great Ocean Road will surprise you. Carved into the cliffside as a memorial to the soldiers who died in World War 1, it runs for 300 spectacular kilometres along the south-west coast of Victoria taking in famous surf beaches, popular holiday resorts, fishing ports and amazing rock sculptures like the Twelve Apostles (right) which were once mainland cliff front. Known in the 19th century as the 'shipwreck coast' — the last sailing ship to bring immigrants to Australia was one of many to founder here with major loss of life — the area has now been dubbed the 'Cappuccino Coast', a reflection of the area's appeal to the gourmet traveller.

TASMANIA

AUSTRALIA'S ONLY ISLAND STATE is a mere 200 kilometres from the mainland. But it remains a world apart. First called Van Diemen's Land — and renowned as the most brutal of penal colonies — Tasmania today is known as the 'heritage isle', the 'apple isle' or the 'holiday isle'. Along with its world-famous wilderness areas, Tasmania's other great attractions are its huge wealth of historical sites and its abundance of gourmet delights.

While Hobart provides a rich taste of Tasmania's diverse charms, there is so much more you can experience on this dramatically beautiful island. And it is all easily accessible. Port Arthur (pictured) on the Tasman Peninsula, once the dumping ground for the colony's most dangerous convicts, is today Tasmania's most popular tourist attraction. The east coast is the driest region of Tasmania. Here you can enjoy fishing, surfing and boating and sample the freshest of seafoods. Famed for the spectacular Cradle Mountain-Lake St Clair National Park, the midlands and central plateau region is also an angler's paradise. In this 'Land of Three Thousand Lakes' you can enjoy world-class trout fishing. A major attraction of a visit to Launceston is driving along the Wine Route, visiting boutique vineyards and tasting some fine vintages.

Traditionally, tourists have been lured here by the rich colonial heritage and the beauty and accessibility of the wilderness areas. Now, Tasmania has added a new appellation to the list — 'the gourmet isle' .

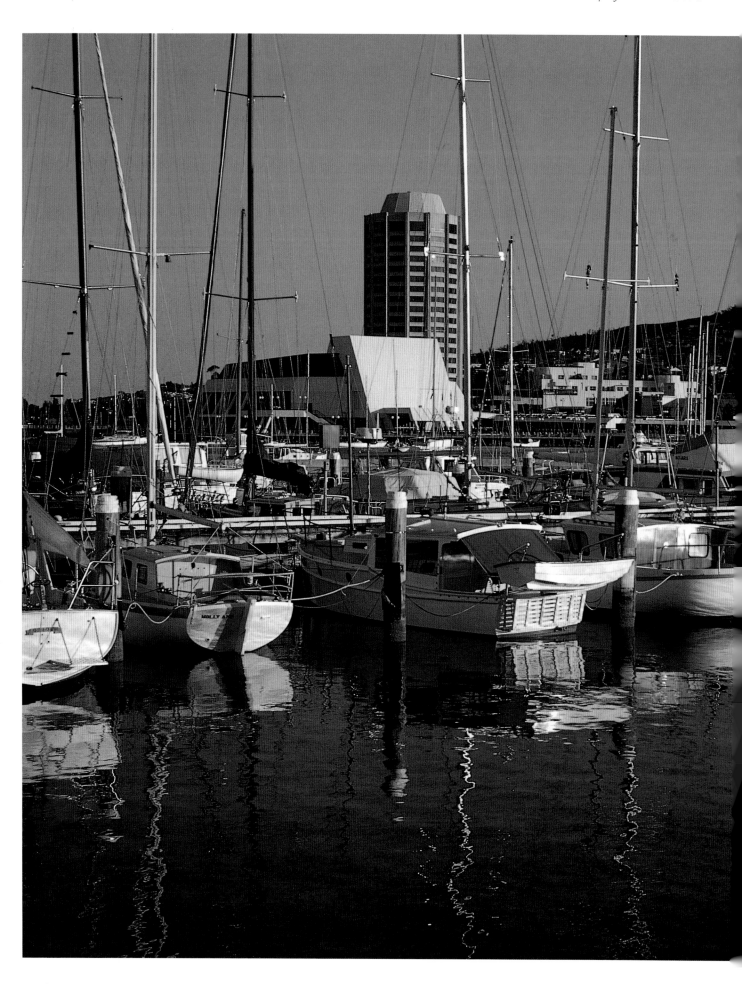

CHAMPAGNE OYSTERS

16 oysters
2 cups coarse rock salt
baby coral lettuce leaves
¼ cup Champagne
2 tablespoons shredded leeks, julienned
¼ cup cream
2 teaspoons lemon juice
salt and pepper
50 g butter
½ lemon cut into wedges

Remove the oysters from their shells. Prepare the shells by putting a mound of salt in the middle of two plates. Sit the empty oyster shells attractively and firmly on the salt. Break the lettuce leaves small enough so that you can line each oyster shell with a little frill sticking over the edge. Put the Champagne into a frying pan and bring to the boil. Add the leek and cook for a few seconds. Put in the oyster meat, shake the pan for 30 seconds until the oysters are warmed. Remove the oysters from the pan using a slotted spoon and keep to one side. Add cream to the liquor in the pan and bring to the boil. Add lemon juice, salt and pepper. Gradually add the butter to the sauce, stirring and shaking the pan continually. Put the oyster meat back into the sauce for a final warm up. As quickly as you can put one oyster covered with its sauce in each shell. Serve with brown bread and lemon wedges.
Serves 2.

MURES UPPER DECK, HOBART, TASMANIA.

Left: The West Point casino overlooks the Hobart waterfront.

BLUE EYE WITH MACADAMIA MAYONNAISE

POTATO MASH
2 large sweet potatoes
2 tablespoons each butter, cream
salt and pepper
MAYONNAISE
1 tablespoon flour
2 egg yolks
1 teaspoon each hot mustard,
white vinegar, lemon juice
500 ml macadamia oil
BLUE EYE
400 g blue eye fillets
salt and pepper
flour
30 g butter

To make sweet potato mash, peel potatoes and cut roughly into small pieces. Place in cold salted water, bring to the boil and simmer for 15 minutes. Remove from heat and drain. Add butter and cream and mash until fluffy. Season to taste. To prepare mayonnaise, make sure all ingredients are at room temperature. Whisk all ingredients except oil in a large bowl. Add the oil in a thin stream, whisking vigorously until the mixture begins to thicken. Add the remaining oil a little at a time, whisking constantly until thick and firm. Add a little warm water if it is too thick. Season. Keep mayonnaise in a cool place covered with plastic film. To serve, remove bones from the blue eye, portion into four nice long pieces. Roll in seasoned flour. Melt butter in a flat-based frying pan over a medium heat. When sizzling add the fish.

Cook for approximately one minute on each side until nicely coloured. Do not overcook. Place mash in the centre of the plate with the fish on top, two pieces per serving. Spoon the macadamia mayonnaise on top of the fish. Can be garnished with roughly chopped macadamia nuts around the edge of the plate.
Serves 2.

MURES UPPER DECK, HOBART, TASMANIA.

Below: The Tasman Bridge arcs gracefully across the Derwent River, linking the city with the eastern suburbs and airport.

A Taste of Heritage

Hobart (left), Australia's second-oldest, smallest and most southerly capital — sits comfortably around a beautiful harbour combining the benefits of a modern city with the rich heritage of its colonial past. Once whaling ships crowded the port. Today, overseas ships berth almost in the city's heart. And every year competitors in the Sydney to Hobart Yacht Race tie up at Constitution Dock for a huge New Year's Eve party thrown by the locals.

For a small city, Hobart offers a surprisingly large number of eating experiences. Local cuisine — such as Champagne Oysters, Blue Eye with Macadamia Mayonnaise and Crispy-Skin Tasman Peninsula Salmon — is a firm favourite. The Docks is a must for lovers of seafood. In addition to the restaurants, cafés and sushi bars, fish punts moored along the dockside offer the catch of the day, freshly unloaded off the boats. Liverpool Street features a range of ethnic cuisines, wholefood and vegetarian dishes. In North Hobart your choices include Italian, Thai, Indian, Indonesian, Lebanese and modern Australian cuisine.

Hobart, with a vibrant restaurant scene and an abundance of fine food and wine, is a gourmet's delight.

King Island Wallaby With Sweet Potato Chips & Raspberry Vinegar

RASPBERRY VINEGAR

1.5 litres white wine vinegar
2 kg fresh raspberries
1 cup brandy
½ cup sugar

2 sweet potatoes
flour
oil
4 farmed wallaby loins
salad leaves
1 punnet fresh raspberries

To make the vinegar, pour the vinegar over 1 kg raspberries. Marinate for 24 hours. Sieve vinegar mixture over the next 1 kg of raspberries. Let marinate for 24 hours. Strain, pushing raspberries through a sieve. Add brandy and sugar to the liquid. Simmer for 1 hour. Do not boil. Skim well. To make the sweet potato chips, first peel the potatoes and then using a vegetable peeler cut wide ribbons off potato. Dust with flour, shake off excess and fry in oil until golden. Char-grill the seasoned wallaby loins until rare. Rest in a warm place until ready to slice. Using a little raspberry vinegar, dress the salad leaves then add some sweet potato chips. Arrange on a plate. Thinly slice the wallaby and arrange on the salad. Top with some sweet potato chips, fresh raspberries and drizzle with more raspberry vinegar.

ROCKERFELLER'S, HOBART, TASMANIA.

VANILLA BEAN & CHOCOLATE BROWNIE ICE-CREAM CAKE WITH BERRIES

VANILLA ICE CREAM

12 egg yolks
1 vanilla bean
1¼ cup castor sugar
½ cup and 2 tablespoons water
2½ cups cream
¼ cup vodka

Beat the yolks in a mixer on high speed. Slice vanilla bean in half lengthwise and scrape out seeds. Boil vanilla bean with sugar and water for 10 minutes. Pour hot syrup into yolks and beat until cool. Whip cream and vodka until soft peaks form. Fold the egg mixture and cream together. Divide into three equal parts. Line a 20 cm springform tin with baking paper 15 cm deep. Pour in one-third ice cream and freeze.

CHOCOLATE BROWNIE

185 g each dark chocolate, unsalted butter
3 eggs
1¾ cups castor sugar
1 teaspoon vanilla essence
1 cup toasted nuts of your choice
1½ tablespoons dark rum
¾ cup plain flour, sifted

Melt chocolate and butter together in a double boiler. Whisk eggs, sugar and vanilla in a bowl until just combined. Fold melted chocolate and egg mixture together. Stir in nuts and rum. Fold in flour. Pour into greased baking tray (40 cm x 30 cm) and bake at 180°C for 20 minutes.

Cool and place in fridge. Cut two circles the size of the cake-tin base out of the brownie and place one on the set ice cream. Pour on another layer of ice cream and freeze. Repeat with remaining brownie and ice cream.

BERRIES

1 punnet each blueberries, raspberries, blackberries
juice of 1 lemon
¹/₂ cup castor sugar

Put all ingredients in a saucepan and bring to the boil. Remove from heat and gently lift out the fruit with a slotted spoon. Reduce the liquid to a syrup. Stir the berries with the syrup and cool.
To serve, place a wedge of ice-cream cake on a cold plate and scatter the berries around it.
Serves 12.

SYRUP, HOBART, TASMANIA.

The neo-Gothic style Convict Church at Port Arthur. Between 1830 and 1877, about 12,500 men and boys served hard time in this most feared of penal settlements. Today, Port Arthur is Tasmania's most popular tourist attraction.

CHOCOLATE MARQUISE

250 g dark cooking chocolate
600 ml King Island pouring cream
375 g sugar
11 egg yolks
500 g butter
250 g cocoa powder
50 g icing sugar

Melt chocolate and cream together over hot water. Beat sugar and egg yolks together until very creamy. Melt butter, and thoroughly mix in cocoa powder and icing sugar. Add to the egg yolk and sugar, stirring constantly. Then add cream and chocolate mixture. Fold all together and freeze in terrines until firm. Serve sliced with seasonal berries and Vanilla Bean Anglaise.
Serves about 10.

'DEAR FRIENDS' LICENSED RESTAURANT, HOBART, TASMANIA.

Wineglass Bay, Freycinet National Park. On a visit to Australia, the Royal yacht Britannia anchored in these beautiful and secluded waters and Queen Elizabeth was treated to an Australian-style barbecue.

BONED CHAR-GRILLED QUAIL WITH TASMANIAN LEATHERWOOD HONEY & GINGER SAUCE

1 Rannoch quail

SAUCE

1 teaspoon minced ginger

1 tablespoon Leatherwood honey

1 cup good quality beef stock

VEGETABLES FOR JULIENNE

carrots

leek

spring onions

red capsicum

Char-grill quail until cooked through. To make sauce, combine all ingredients and reduce by half. Add quail at the last moment to glaze. Cut quail through the centre and place halves on blanched julienne of vegetables. Serves 1.

'DEAR FRIENDS' LICENSED RESTAURANT, HOBART, TASMANIA.

Below: Launceston, Australia's third-oldest city and the commercial centre of northern Tasmania, is also an ideal base for your exploration of the Wine Route.

ALMOND TUILLE WITH THREE ICE CREAMS & SPUN TOFFEE

TUILLE MIX
4 egg whites

200 g castor sugar

100 g flour

75 g ground almonds

150 g butter, melted

BERRY COULIS
1 punnet each strawberries, raspberries,

blueberries

½ cup port

¼ cup sugar

SPUN SUGAR
500 g sugar

250 ml water

To prepare the tuille mix, whisk egg whites and sugar until frothy, fold in remaining ingredients. Spread thin 10 cm discs of dough out on a lightly greased tray and bake at 240°C for 5 minutes. Pull out and drape tuille over an inverted cup until set. To make the berry coulis, blend all ingredients in a food processor. To prepare the spun sugar, boil the sugar and water rapidly until mixture starts to turn golden. Set aside. When toffee starts to ribbon, using a fork 'spin' strands of toffee over a pole, going back and forth until a good band of strands are spun. Shape into a cylinder. To serve, place a pool of coulis then the tuille on a plate. Fill the tuille with three scoops of Sticky Fingers ice cream and then the spun toffee. Dust with icing sugar.

Serves 8.

ROCKERFELLER'S, HOBART, TASMANIA.

WILD EXPERIENCES

Tasmania embraces a greater percentage of protected wilderness than any other Australian state. World Heritage listed areas take up some 20 percent alone. Even in a few days you can enjoy a surprising number of the 'wilderness experiences' that help make Tasmania unique.

Lying in the central north and covering some of the state's highest and most spectacular country, the Cradle Mountain-Lake St Clair National Park (right) is Tasmania's most famous wilderness area and a bushwalkers' mecca. The 85 kilometre Overland Track is one of Australia's best-known walking routes. The adjoining Franklin-Gordon Wild Rivers National Park attracts wilderness adventurers from around the world to test themselves against its extremely hazardous white waters. Maria Island National Park, off the east coast, is unique. This is the only park where you can see eleven of the state's native bird species. Forester kangaroos, emus and Cape Barren geese are a common sight on this peaceful island. The Southwest National Park encompasses rugged mountains, dense rainforest, tranquil lakes and a jagged, treacherous coast. Often swept by storms but always breathtakingly beautiful, it is the largest jewel in Tasmania's wilderness heritage crown.

CRISPY-SKIN TASMAN PENINSULA SALMON WITH HERB COUSCOUS, SNOW PEAS & SAFFRON BUTTER

COUSCOUS

250 g couscous
chopped herbs – parsley, oregano, thyme
1 teaspoon butter

SAFFRON BUTTER

2 each oranges, lemons
zest of 1 lemon
¾ cup white wine vinegar
5 peppercorns
2 bay leaves
pinch saffron threads
5 egg yolks
300 g clarified butter

4 skinned and boned salmon steaks
500 g snow peas, top and tailed
1 leek, cut in julienne strips
oil for frying

To prepare the couscous, place it in a bowl and add 1 cup boiling water. Cover for 5 minutes. Mix in herbs and butter and fluff up with a fork. Microwave to reheat. To prepare the saffron butter, chop up the oranges and lemons, place in a saucepan with the lemon zest, vinegar, peppercorns and bay leaves. Bring to the boil and reduce by half. Remove from heat, add the saffron threads and let steep for 30 minutes. In a large bowl over a double boiler whisk the eggs and the strained vinegar mixture until it starts to thicken. Remove from heat and slowly whisk in the clarified butter. Pan-cook the seasoned salmon, skin side down, until the skin is crispy. Flip over for 2 minutes.

Arrange the couscous in a pile in the middle of the plate. Pour sauce around the outside. Arrange cooked hot snow peas on top then the piece of salmon. Lastly, top with julienned leek which has been fried in oil until crispy.

ROCKERFELLER'S, HOBART, TASMANIA.

Below: An angler's paradise by any standards, Tasmania is famous for three species of fish: trout of world-class size in fresh water, bream in the estuaries and tuna off the coast.

Following pages 96 & 97: Russell Falls, Mount Field National Park — a taste of the famous Tasmanian wilderness, just over an hour's drive from Hobart.

GOATS' CHEESE &
EGGPLANT PASTRY STACK

BAKED EGGPLANT
2 eggplants
2 cloves garlic
2 tablespoons plain yoghurt
juice of 1/2 lemon

TOMATO CONCASSE
6 fresh tomatoes
1 onion
2 cloves garlic
2 basil leaves, chopped

4 zucchini, sliced
2 red capsicums, sliced
300 g puff pastry
8 slices Bothwell goats' cheese

Bake eggplant in oven until soft then
blend with garlic, yoghurt and lemon
juice. To make the tomato concasse,
combine and cook ingredients to a
sauce consistency. Grill the zucchini
and capsicums. Roll out puff pastry into
a thin layer. Bake and cut into shapes.
To assemble, layer pastry, cheese and
vegetables, heat in oven for 20-30
minutes. Place some sauce on plate.
Place 'stack' on top and sprinkle with
chopped parsley.

Serves 4.

PANACHE, HOBART, TASMANIA.

SOUTH AUSTRALIA

SOUTH AUSTRALIA has always been different from the other states. It was the only colony to be established without the aid of convict labour. It is the driest state in the driest continent. Beyond the spectacular Flinders Ranges (pictured) there is little but desert for thousands of kilometres. In the world's most urbanised country, it is the most urbanised of states, with the vast majority of its inhabitants living in the fertile south-east corner, centred on Adelaide.

But this is also the 'festival state' — the Adelaide Festival of Arts, the Barossa Valley Vintage Festival, Schutzenfest, the Greek Glendi Festival and the Cornish Kernewek Lowender — here people enjoy making the most of life. Fittingly, South Australia is the country's leading wine-producing state. And a state fit for gourmets.

From the historic sun-bleached towns along the mighty Murray River to the untamed, wild south-east coast; from the lush wine country of the Barossa Valley, to the harsh desert country of the north; from the loneliness of the mighty Nullarbor Plain to the elegant nightlife of Adelaide — South Australia is remarkably varied. And different.

ROAST SPLIT MARRON WITH SPICED ROCKMELON & MUNTRIES SALSA

2 live marrons
100 g butter
2 tablespoons lemon juice
salt and pepper
1 rockmelon
2 cups orange juice, strained
6 tablespoons each rice wine vinegar,
sugar
1 stick lemon grass, bruised
2 chillies, seeded and chopped
100 g fresh muntries
¾ cup extra virgin olive oil

Chill marron, split in half and clean. Melt butter, add lemon juice, season and brush marron well. Cut rockmelon in small cubes. Bring juice, vinegar, sugar, lemon grass and chillies to the boil for 5 minutes. Pour mixture over melon and muntries. Cool, then add oil. Mix well. Roast marron on high heat until shells are red, preferably over open char flame, basting with more butter as needed.

Serves 2.

RED OCHRE GRILL, ADELAIDE, SOUTH AUSTRALIA.

Adelaide — Australia's most gracious city.

Sautéed Prawns With Roast Sweet Potato, Red Wine Reduction & Basil Oil

RED WINE REDUCTION

1 each carrot, onion, peeled and diced

1 red capsicum, seeded and diced

2 cloves garlic, peeled

1 tablespoon oil

4 Roma tomatoes, roughly chopped

2 cups port

750 ml Cabernet Sauvignon

BASIL OIL

1 cup vegetable oil

2 bunches basil (reserve 4 nice pieces for garnish)

20 prawns, peeled and de-veined

oil

500 g sweet potato, cubed and roasted

To make the red wine reduction, sauté carrot, onion, capsicum and garlic in oil in a medium-sized saucepan for 2 minutes. Add tomatoes, port and red wine and reduce on low heat for 30 minutes. Remove from heat and strain, pushing some of the solids through to give the reduction body. Set aside. To prepare the basil oil, process all ingredients in a food processor. Stand for 30 minutes and decant off coloured and flavoured oil. Set aside. To prepare prawns and sweet potato, sauté prawns in some oil until just cooked, approximately 5 minutes. Keep warm. Warm sweet potato in the oven.

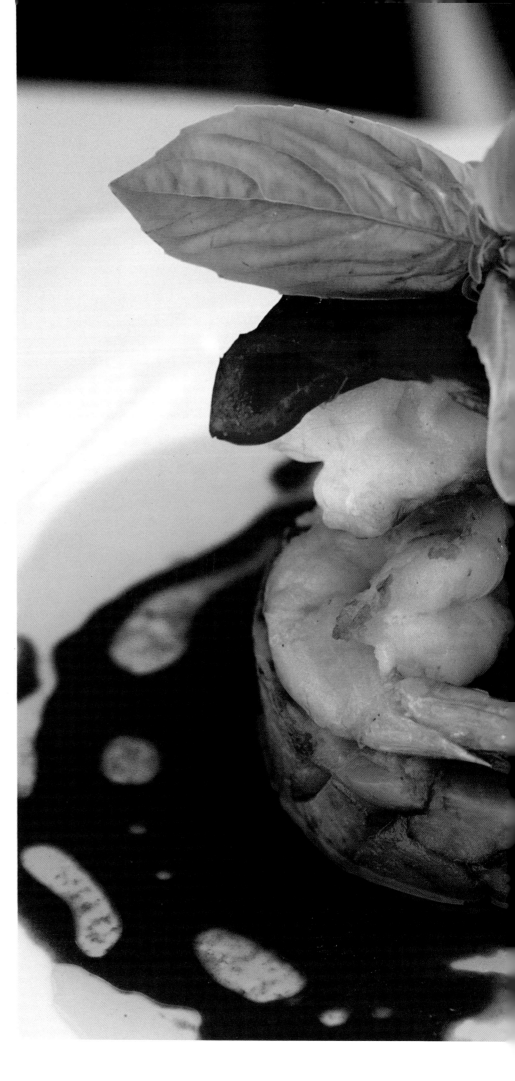

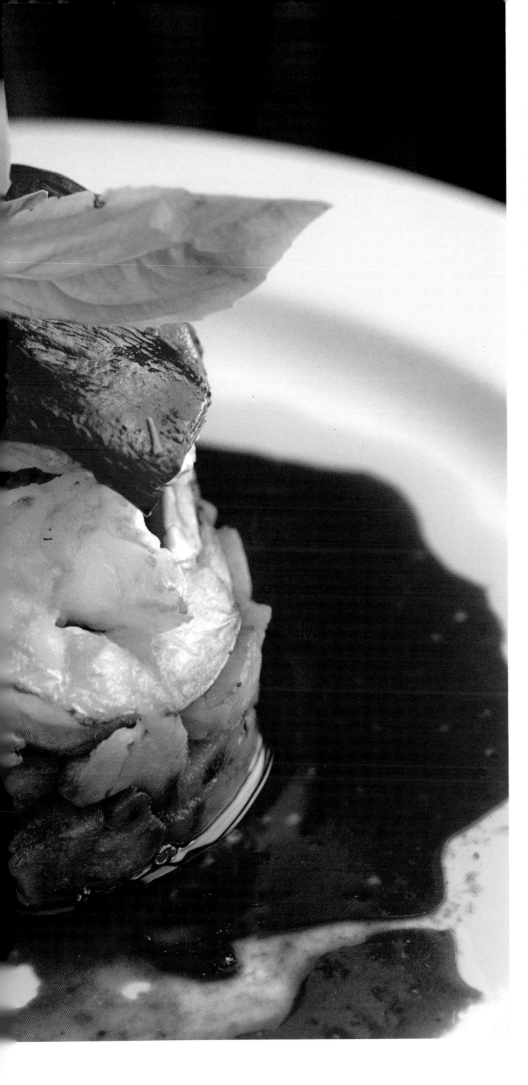

To assemble, divide sweet potato into four serves and place in the centre of four warmed plates. Place 5 prawns per plate on top of the sweet potato. Spoon 3 tablespoons per plate of the red wine reduction around the sweet potato and prawns. Repeat with basil oil and garnish with basil leaves. Serves 4.

CAON'S, ADELAIDE, SOUTH AUSTRALIA.

WILD LIME LAMINGTON

WILD LIME SYRUP

juice of 20 wild limes
1 tablespoon each castor sugar, lemon juice

Combine ingredients and bring to boil. Reduce heat and simmer for 5 minutes. Purée in food processor or blender.

MANGO SORBET

³/₄ cup water
100 g castor sugar
2 cups mango pulp

Boil water and sugar for 5 minutes. Cool. Add mango pulp and purée. Freeze in an ice-cream machine.

SPONGE

¹/₂ cup and 2 tablespoons castor sugar
5 eggs
1 tablespoon butter
¹/₄ cup wild lime syrup
2¹/₄ cups cake flour

500 g white chocolate
250 g shredded coconut

Pre-heat oven to 200°C. Whisk sugar and eggs over a water bath to 45°C, remove from heat and whisk to room temperature. Melt butter and add to wild lime syrup. Fold well-sieved flour into egg mixture. Add lime/butter syrup. Pour mixture into greased and lined lamington tin 25 cm x 13 cm. Bake at 200°C for 20-25 minutes or until cake springs back to touch.Cut into 6 pieces, dip sponge into melted white chocolate, roll in coconut threads, serve with mango sorbet and chocolate sauce.

Serves 6.

RED OCHRE GRILL, ADELAIDE, SOUTH AUSTRALIA.

GRACIOUS LIVING

Set between the rolling hills of the Mount Lofty Ranges and the blue waters of Gulf St Vincent, Adelaide is perhaps the most gracious of all the Australian capitals, combining the vitality of a large modern city — population around one million — with an easygoing lifestyle. More thought went into the siting of Adelaide than any other Australian capital, making it a civilized, human-scale place to live. It is the only major world city completely surrounded by parklands.

Adelaide prides itself on providing the good things in life and boasts more restaurants per head of population than any other city in Australia. Given the huge variety of dishes to be found — including Roast Split Marron with Spiced Rockmelon & Muntries Salsa; Hot & Sour Yabbies; Kangaroo Carpaccio & Sesame Sauce; and Whole Fried Salt & Pepper Barramundi with Stir-fried Bok Choy — deciding where to begin can be difficult. Hindley Street offers a great choice of ethnic eateries including Italian, Lebanese and Greek, along with trendy brasseries and cafés. Rundle Street East has a distinctly Mediterranean flavour, including Greek, Spanish and Italian dishes. Gouger Street lays claim to having one of the highest concentrations and diversity of restaurants in any single street in Australia.

LAMBS' BRAINS WITH HOLLANDAISE

COURT BOUILLON
2 cups water

1/2 cup white wine

1/4 cup white vinegar

2 bay leaves

8 black peppercorns

1 each onion, carrot, celery stick,
chopped

HOLLANDAISE
4 egg yolks

2 tablespoons white wine vinegar

350 g clarified butter, melted

ONE SERVING
3 brain lobes

homemade breadcrumbs

vegetable oil or clarified butter

6 baby spinach leaves

1/4 - 1/2 cup hollandaise

1/4 cup beef glaze

To prepare the Court Bouillon, bring all ingredients to the boil for 5 minutes. To make the Hollandaise Sauce, whisk together egg yolks and vinegar over low heat until light and fluffy. Slowly add the butter until sauce has thickened and all the butter is combined. To cook the brains, poach brains in Court Bouillon for 10 minutes, allow to cool in the liquid. Drain the brains. Crumb in homemade breadcrumbs and shallow-fry in either vegetable oil or clarified butter until golden brown all over. Cook spinach in boiling salted water for 15 seconds and drain on a dry cloth for 30 seconds. Place the Hollandaise in the centre of a plate. Surround with warm glaze.

Put spinach in centre of Hollandaise and place brain lobes on 3 sides, facing vertically.

JOLLEYS BOATHOUSE RESTAURANT, ADELAIDE, SOUTH AUSTRALIA.

Page 105: St Peter's Cathedral, Adelaide, which boasts the finest and biggest bells in the Southern Hemisphere.

BEEF WITH RED PESTO

RED PESTO

100 g sundried tomatoes
50 g semi-dried tomatoes
1 clove garlic
100 g roasted capsicum, peeled
2 tablespoons grated Parmesan cheese
2 tablespoons pine nuts, roasted and chopped
salt and pepper

BALSAMIC DRESSING

100 ml balsamic vinegar
200 ml olive oil
1/2 teaspoon whole grain mustard

HASH BROWNS

4 teaspoons plain flour
4 cups grated potato
1 cup chopped onion
1/2 teaspoon salt
olive oil

200 g cooked spinach
4 x 250 g beef fillets

To make the red pesto, purée sundried tomatoes, garlic and capsicum in a food processor. Fold in cheese and pine nuts and season. To make the balsamic dressing, mix together all ingredients with a whisk. To make the hash browns, mix all ingredients together and fry in four cakes in a thick-based pan in a little olive oil until golden on both sides. Use an egg ring for convenience. To assemble, place hash browns in the centre of serving plates. Put spinach on top of hash browns and place beef on top. Pour dressing over the beef then finally place 1 tablespoon of red pesto on top. Serves 4.

JOLLEYS BOATHOUSE RESTAURANT, ADELAIDE, SOUTH AUSTRALIA.

WHOLE FRIED SALT & PEPPER BARRAMUNDI WITH STIR-FRIED BOK CHOY

1 barramundi
white pepper
salt
Sichuan pepper
rice flour
oil for deep frying
½ bok choy
2 tablespoons sesame oil
1 fried potato croûton

Clean and score barramundi. Rub with salt and pepper mix (white pepper, salt, Sichuan pepper). Dip in rice flour and deep-fry until crispy, approximately 5 minutes. Stir-fry washed and halved bok choy in sesame oil.

To serve, place barramundi on fried potato croûton and sit bok choy on top.

Serves 1.

UNIVERSAL WINE BAR, ADELAIDE, SOUTH AUSTRALIA.

WINE CAPITAL

South Australia produces about 50 percent of the wines and 65 percent of the brandy made in Australia. The state has seven distinct grape-growing regions — the Barossa, McLaren Vale, Clare Valley, Riverland, the Adelaide Hills, Coonawarra and Langhorne Creek.

The Barossa Valley — Australia's most famous wine-producing area is located about 55 kilometres north-east of Adelaide. Today the area has a distinctive culture and atmosphere that derives from the Germanic concentration in the mid-nineteenth century.

The Barossa produces dry and sweet table wines and brandy. There are several medium-sized wineries producing excellent wines and some boutique wineries specializing in a limited market.

The McLaren Vale region — situated on the Fleurieu Peninsula just south of Adelaide and particularly suitable for red wines. There are more

*Pages 108-109: Barossa Valley vineyards.
This is Australia's most famous
wine-producing area.*

*Left: A Barossa winery. The mid-nineteenth
century Germanic influence is evidenced in
the architecture of the area.*

than 50 wineries in the region ranging from the very large to the very small.

The Clare Valley — located about 130 kilometres north of Adelaide. There are 28 wineries, most of which are small family-owned operations, specializing in Semillon, Shiraz and Reisling.

The Riverland region — situated near the Victorian border. The wineries here produce a wide range of products from table wines to ouzo and brandy.

The Adelaide Hills — there are numerous vineyards scattered throughout the area. A noted specialty is Riesling.

Langhorne Creek — a rapidly expanding wine region about 70 kilometres south of Adelaide, producing mostly reds.

Coonawarra — located in the far south-east of the state and known for award-winning white and red table wines.

South Australia is the nation's wine capital.

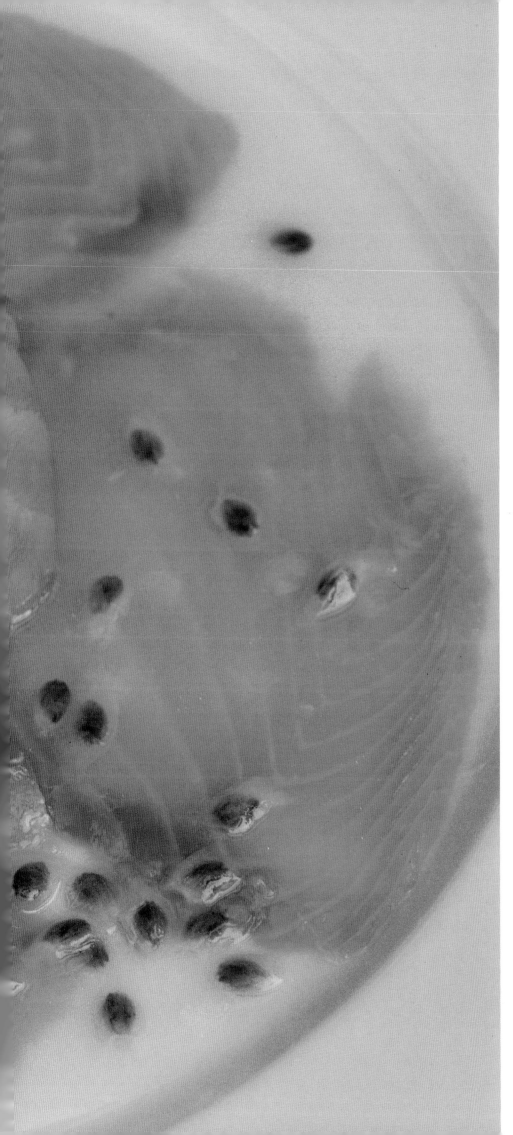

SPRING SMOKED SALMON WITH PASSIONFRUIT & ORANGE DRESSING & YOUNG SALAD GREENS

DRESSING

2 tablespoons orange juice
juice of 1/2 lemon
2 tablespoons extra virgin olive oil
pulp of 2 passionfruit
1/2 teaspoon sugar
salt and pepper

1 cup mixed salad lettuces
4 slices smoked salmon
chopped chives

To make the dressing, place orange juice, lemon juice, olive oil, passionfruit and sugar in a bowl and whisk together. Add salt and pepper to taste. Place the salad lettuces in the centre of a plate and lay smoked salmon slices over the top in a cross shape, pour over dressing and garnish with chopped chives.
Serves 1.

CAON'S, ADELAIDE, SOUTH AUSTRALIA.

114

HOT & SOUR YABBIES

3 each red onions, red capsicums,
roughly chopped
1 tablespoon chopped fresh root ginger
6 splashes each fish sauce,
rice wine vinegar
1½-1¾ cups mirin
2 tablespoons each Tom Yum paste,
sugar
juice of 2 lemons, 2 limes
½ bunch each basil, coriander
6 yabbies, halved and deep fried
mesclun mix

Sauté onion, capsicums and ginger.
Add fish sauce, rice wine vinegar,
mirin, Tom Yum, sugar, lemon and
lime juice. Purée in a food processor
with basil and coriander. Toss yabbies
with dressing and mesclun mix.
Serves 6.

UNIVERSAL WINE BAR,
ADELAIDE, SOUTH AUSTRALIA.

The fertile south-east of Australia's
driest state.

OYSTERS WITH SALSA OF MANGO, CUCUMBER & CHILLI

24 oysters in shell
SALSA
200 g cucumber, chopped
250 g chopped mango
1 small chilli, chopped
1/4 bunch coriander
2 tablespoons rice wine vinegar
1 tablespoon mirin

Ensure oysters are clean. Mix all salsa ingredients together in a bowl. Top oysters with 1 teaspoon of salsa. To serve, stack one on top of another in the centre of a plate. Serves 4.

JOLLEYS BOATHOUSE RESTAURANT, ADELAIDE, SOUTH AUSTRALIA.

Right: The 'Remarkable Rocks', Kangaroo Island. Spectacular geographical formations and an amazing variety of native fauna and flora are features of Australia's third-largest island.

Left: The spectacular Flinders Ranges.

THAI BEEF SALAD

DRESSING

¹/₂ bunch each basil, mint, coriander, parsley

3 cloves garlic

¹/₂ stick lemon grass

1 teaspoon each Tom Yum paste, brown sugar

1 tablespoon grated root ginger

3 tablespoons each fish sauce, oil, vinegar

SALAD

100 g toasted peanuts

100 g rice vermicelli, soaked

snow pea shoots

lettuce

coriander

bean shoots

red capsicum, sliced

400 g beef sirloin, roasted rare and rested

To prepare the dressing, wash all herbs thoroughly. Place all ingredients in a blender and blend to a smooth paste. To assemble, mix all the salad ingredients in a bowl, pour over the dressing, arrange neatly in the middle of a plate and lay the sliced beef on top.
Serves 4.

BOLTZ CAFÉ & BAR, ADELAIDE, SOUTH AUSTRALIA.

KANGAROO CARPACCIO & SESAME SAUCE

SESAME SAUCE
2 tablespoons sesame seeds
¼ cup castor sugar
1½ tablespoons mirin
1 tablespoon Kikkoman Soy Sauce

100 g kangaroo saddle
2 teaspoons Cajun spices
olive oil

To prepare the sauce, dry-toast sesame seeds in a cast iron wok at 200°C for 20 minutes, stir a few times to avoid excess burning around the edges. Let cool on a tray for 30 minutes. (Never use burnt seeds for this dish.) Grind them in a mortar and pestle with sugar until very smooth, it may take 30 minutes. Do not use a food processor. Do not add any liquid at this stage until the paste is smooth. Finally add mirin and soy into the paste. It stores very well in the refrigerator; it may need more mirin as the paste thickens through time. To prepare the kangaroo, trim all sinews from the meat, pat dry. Coat all over with Cajun spices (obtained by mail from Don's Table). Dry-fry in a heavy skillet for a total of 3 minutes on all sides; do not overcook the meat, it should be rare. Cool on a tray, let meat set half-frozen in a -10°C freezer for 4 hours. Cut into slices 2 mm thick, fan them out on a clean plate. Drizzle sesame sauce and good olive oil on top and garnish with well dressed salad leaves.

Serves 10.

DON'S TABLE, ADELAIDE, SOUTH AUSTRALIA.

ANCIENT SPLENDOUR

Running north from Gulf St Vincent for 400 kilometres into the arid outback, the Flinders Ranges (right) possess a stark, timeless beauty. This is a superb area for bushwalking. In the early mornings and evenings, you have a good chance of spotting wildlife including emus and kangaroos. The birdlife is prolific.

The best-known feature of the Flinders Ranges is Wilpena Pound, one of the most extraordinary geological formations in Australia. A vast oval rock bowl covering 50 square kilometres, the Pound is surrounded by sheer cliffs rising to 1000 metres. The only entrance is through a narrow gorge. Within the Pound are hills and ridges and a wonderland of birdlife — rosellas, galahs, red-capped robins, budgerigars and wedgetailed eagles are common.

The ruggedness of the Flinders Ranges holds a great attraction for film-makers. This magnificent landscape has appeared in *Sunday Too Far Away*, *The Lighthorsemen* and *Gallipoli*.

ONKAPARINGA VALLEY VENISON WITH RED CURRANT SAUCE

RED CURRANT SAUCE

¹/₄-¹/₂ cup sugar
250 g frozen red currants
1 cup each red wine, spring water

150 g trimmed venison, loin or rump
salt and pepper
oil
¹/₄ cup red currant sauce
100 g black-peppered pasta, cooked

To prepare the sauce, caramelise the sugar slowly, add currants, red wine and water. Bring to the boil and cook until sugar is dissolved, 5-10 minutes.

Cool sauce and blend in a food processor. Strain through a fine sieve.

Return to stove and bring back to boiling point. To prepare the venison, season with salt and pepper and sear in hot oil on both sides. Roast in the oven for 3-5 minutes (to cook medium rare). Remove from oven and rest meat for 2-3 minutes then cut into thin slices. Place cooked pasta in the middle of a serving plate and place meat on top. Drizzle sauce around the outside of the plate.

Garnish if desired.

Sauce serves about 8.

Meat serves 1.

THE MANSE, NORTH ADELAIDE, SOUTH AUSTRALIA.

TURKEY IN MOLE POBLANO

CHILE PURÉE

8 mulatto chillies
5 ancho chillies
6 pasilla chillies
4 tablespoons lard

Slit the chillies open and remove the seeds and membranes. Reserve 1 tablespoon of seeds. Put the chillies in a bowl of hot water and let soak for at least 20 minutes until soft then discard the water and blend them with only enough water to make the blending work in two batches. Melt the lard in a deep pan and fry the puréed chillies for about 10 minutes, stirring to ensure they do not catch.

SPICE NUT & TOMATILLO MIXTURE

6 tomatillos
Dry Spices — 6 cloves, 10 peppercorns,
1/2 stick cinnamon crushed, 1/2 teaspoon
coriander seeds and the reserved chilli
seeds
7 tablespoons sesame seeds

Toast all ingredients except sesame seeds in a dry pan and finely grind in a spice grinder. Toast sesame seeds separately in a dry pan, stirring until golden. Grind separately.

SAUCE

2 tablespoons raisins
20 almonds, skin on, roughly chopped
1/2 cup pepitas (hulled pumpkin seeds)
2 stale corn tortillas, torn up (fry the
tortillas until crisp)
chocolate
4-5 cups turkey stock

Put all the ingredients (not including the lard) into the blender and blend to make a thick mixture, adding as much turkey stock as you need to let the blender work. Blend until fine. To complete the sauce, add the blended tomatillo, spice and nut mixture to the chilli purée, and cook for about 5 minutes, stirring. Add one tablet of chocolate cut into its segments, and stir until it is melted. Add 4-5 cups of turkey stock, and keep cooking for about 20 minutes, stirring occasionally to ensure it does not catch or stick.

TURKEY

1 kg turkey pieces, cubed
egg white
cornflour
oil

To cook the turkey in the mole, toss turkey pieces in a slurry of egg white and cornflour. Plunge the turkey pieces into hot oil for 10 seconds. This should seal them without creating any thick batter. Poach the turkey pieces in the mole for 20 minutes at a slight simmer. Serve with rice and a purée of sweet corn, finely diced red capsicum, finely diced pumpkin, moistened with a little milk and livened with chilli serrano.
Serves 6.

DON'S TABLE, ADELAIDE,
SOUTH AUSTRALIA.

Left: Coober Pedy, in the heart of South Australia's outback, is the world's richest opal field. Over half the population live underground to escape the searing heat which can reach 50°C.
Inset: A subterranean church.

ROASTED GARLIC & ANCHOVY BAVAROIS WITH OCTOPUS AIOLI, ALMOND & ANCHOVY TUILLE, COUSCOUS & PARSLEY & A BEETROOT & SAFFRON DRESSING

BAVAROIS

2¹/₂ cups buttermilk
blended anchovy and roasted garlic
to taste
³/₄ cup cream
5 leaves gelatine
³/₄ cup whipped cream
white pepper

Warm buttermilk, anchovy and garlic.
Add cream and gelatine. Cool.
Fold in whipped cream. Add pepper.
Place in six to eight moulds.
Chill for 24 hours.

AIOLI

50 g octopus tentacles
1 tablespoon tomato paste
garlic and seasoning to taste
2 eggs
2 cups oil

Roast octopus with tomato paste for
15 minutes or until cooked. Purée
with garlic and seasoning. Make aioli
by blending eggs on high speed and
slowly adding oil. Fold in octopus.
Re-season to taste
(juice of 1 lemon optional).

COUSCOUS & PARSLEY

250 g couscous
1 Spanish onion, finely diced
1 teaspoon diced garlic
1 tomato, finely diced
1 bunch parsley, finely diced
lemon juice and seasoning to taste

Cook couscous according to packet instructions. Allow to cool and combine with all ingredients.

ALMOND TUILLE

250 g butter
¹/₄ cup sugar
¹/₂ teaspoon salt
150 g flour
125 g ground almonds
¹/₄ teaspoon each chilli paste,
crushed garlic
6 egg whites

Cream butter and sugar. Add remaining ingredients (except egg whites). Beat on high for 10 minutes, slowly add egg whites until mixture comes together. Spread in thin circles on baking paper and bake at 150°C until golden brown.

BEETROOT & SAFFRON DRESSING

¹/₂ cup each sugar, water
¹/₄ teaspoon saffron strands

Bring mixture to boil. Simmer until mixture coats back of spoon. Cool and strain.

¹/₂ cup sugar
³/₄ cup water
250 g peeled and diced beetroot

Bring sugar and water to the boil. Cook beetroot until tender and syrup thickens. Cool and strain. To serve, unmould bavarois onto serving plates. Serve with aioli, couscous, almond tuille and dressing.
Serves 6-8.

THE OXFORD, NORTH ADELAIDE, SOUTH AUSTRALIA.

WESTERN AUSTRALIA

VAST IMMENSE. A big land with big attractions. Sprawling across a third of the continent, Western Australia is the largest of the Australian States and Territories with less than one-tenth of the nation's population. Perth (pictured) is closer to Jakarta than Canberra and is the most isolated city of its size in the world. In the wide open spaces of Western Australia, people are as rare as rain with 80 percent of the state's 1.5 million inhabitants clustered in and around the capital in the south-west.

Aptly described as the garden of Western Australia, the southern corner of the State is a world of towering jarrah and karri forests, lush green countryside dotted with farms and orchards. And the burgeoning vineyards of the Margaret River region. To the north-east, and 600 kilometres from Perth, is Kalgoorlie-Boulder. At the height of its gold rush days, Kalgoorlie's 'Golden Mile' was the richest piece of real estate in the world. It still produces 70 percent of the gold mined in Australia and retains the atmosphere of a frontier mining town.

Drive north up the coast from Perth and you will discover magnificent beaches, excellent fishing and coral reefs. And some of the country's best seafood. Inland lies the hallucinatory world of the great deserts. The Outback beyond the Outback.

In Western Australia, nature rules.

ROAST FILLET OF BIODYNAMIC BEEF WITH POTATO MASH & OLIVE PURÉE

POTATO MASH
3 large Foxton potatoes
cream
OLIVE PURÉE
100 g Kalamata olives, pitted
1 tablespoon capers
1 teaspoon Dijon mustard
olive oil

250 g biodynamic eye fillet
½ cup beef jus
watercress for garnish

To prepare the potato mash, boil and purée potatoes, add cream until right consistency. To prepare the olive purée, blend olives, capers and Dijon mustard together. At the last minute add olive oil for sheen. Sear fillet and bake until medium rare. To serve, cut fillet in half and serve on potato mash with a teaspoon of olive purée, sauce with beef jus and garnish with watercress.
Serves 1.

FRASER'S RESTAURANT, WEST PERTH, WESTERN AUSTRALIA.

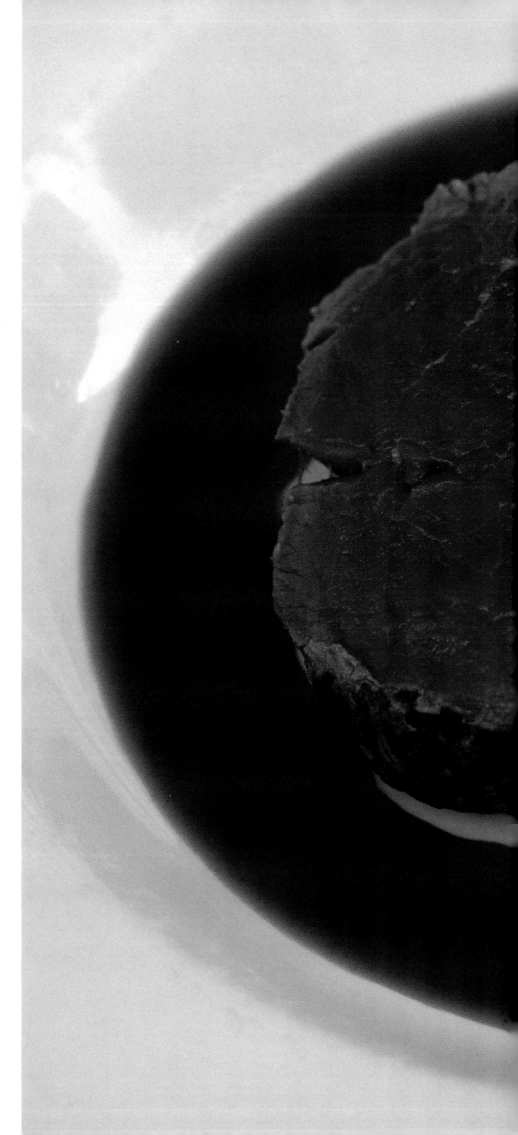

ROAST LAMB RACK, GARLIC POTATOES, SPINACH & MINT JUS

HERB OIL
1 clove garlic
¼ bunch mint (reserve some for jus)
¼ cup olive oil
100 g rocket leaves
few sprigs Italian parsley

LAMB RACK
1.2 kg lamb rack, trimmed and bones cleaned

GARLIC POTATOES
4 Chat potatoes
2 cloves garlic
1 sprig fresh thyme
2 tablespoons olive oil
salt and pepper

MINT JUS
1 tablespoon red wine vinegar
¼ cup veal or lamb jus

200 g English spinach

To prepare herb oil, place all ingredients in a food processor. Allow to settle for 24 hours and decant. Season and roast lamb racks in a hot oven, 220°C until pink. Rest in a warm place. Reserve jus and mix with a little mint.

SUNSHINE CUISINE

Set on the banks of the sparkling Swan River, Perth enjoys a superb climate. And culinary choices to match. Our featured dishes — including Salmon Gravlax; Red Curry of Blue Manna Crab, Bok Choy & Jasmine Rice; and Coconut Prawns with Spiced Mango Chutney — are just a sample of the gourmet delights available in this city of space and light.

Northbridge, a major centre of Perth's migrant population and nightlife, has one of the biggest concentrations of restaurants in Australia, with the emphasis on international cuisine. Fremantle, Perth's port, is a natural for alfresco dining.

To prepare garlic potatoes, roast potatoes with the rest of the ingredients. To assemble, toss spinach through potato mixture and sauté lightly. Place on the base of each plate. Slice lamb into cutlets, serve four per plate. Drizzle jus over, add a few drops of herb oil and red wine vinegar. Accompany with a glass of Voyager Estate Cabernet Merlot 1993 (Margaret River).
Serves 4.

NO.44 KING STREET, PERTH, WESTERN AUSTRALIA.

Left: Perth, Australia's most isolated capital, stands confidently on the banks of the Swan River.
Below: Cottesloe Beach. Perth's Indian Ocean surfing beaches rank among the best in Australia.

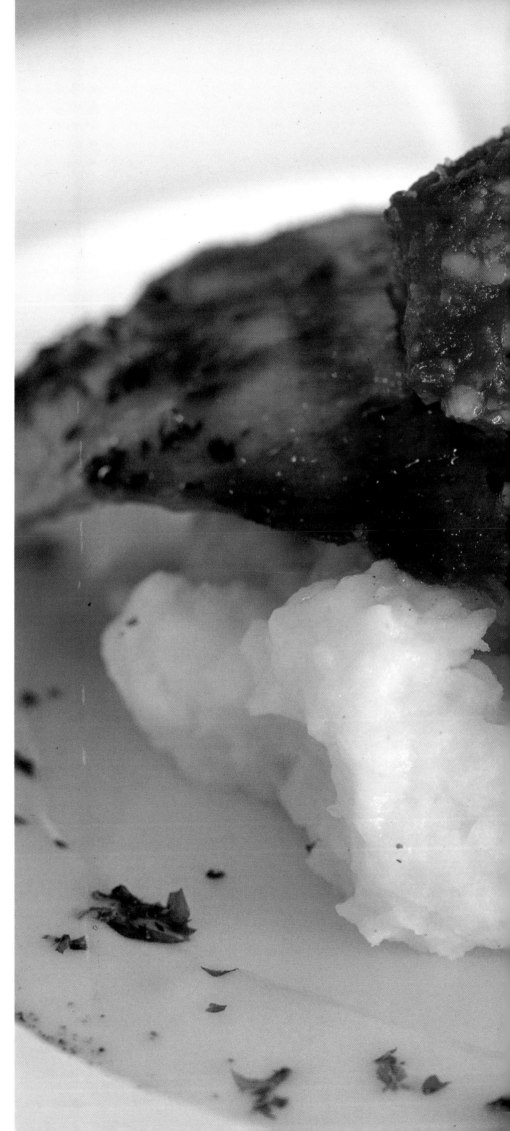

SALMON GRAVLAX

SALMON GRAVLAX

(3 days) 1/4 cup each rock salt, juniper
berries, sugar, dessert wine
1 tablespoon black pepper
1/4 cup chopped dill
1 kg raw side of salmon

SEEDED MUSTARD
VINAIGRETTE

100 ml olive oil
1 1/2 tablespoons sherry vinegar
2 tablespoons seeded wine mustard
1 teaspoon crushed garlic
salt and pepper
2 Ciabatta (olive oil loaf) wafers
1 1/2 tablespoons olive tapenade
rocket leaves
80 g gravlax
2 1/2 tablespoons seeded mustard vinaigrette

GARNISH

fennel
shredded beetroot

Blitz the rock salt and berries in a food processor then add the remaining ingredients to form a paste. Spread paste evenly over the salmon then cover and refrigerate. The next day turn the salmon over and place back in the fridge. On the third day the salmon is ready to slice and serve. Combine ingredients for dressing. To assemble, brush Ciabatta wafers with the olive tapenade and grill until golden brown. Place rocket leaves on the base of the plate and arrange the salmon gravlax on top. Dress the salmon with the vinaigrette and arrange on the plate. Garnish with wafers, fennel and beetroot. Serves 6-8.

COCO'S, SOUTH PERTH,
WESTERN AUSTRALIA.

RED CURRY OF BLUE MANNA CRAB, BOK CHOY & JASMINE RICE

RED CURRY PASTE

3 dried red chillies

1 red onion

4-6 cloves garlic

1/2 tablespoon each chopped lemon grass, galangal

1 tablespoon chopped coriander root

1 teaspoon each cumin seeds, coriander seeds

1 clove

1 1/2 teaspoons each salt, Thai shrimp paste, chopped kaffir lime leaf

1/2 teaspoon each mace, nutmeg

SAUCE

red curry paste (as above)

350 ml coconut milk

750 ml to 1 litre chicken stock

1 teaspoon each palm sugar, fish sauce

4 kaffir lime leaves

juice of 1 lime

CRAB

4 to 6 (approximately 1 kg) blue manna crabs, cleaned

1 bunch bok choy

GARNISH

2 tablespoons chopped coriander

1-2 red chillies, according to taste

ACCOMPANIMENT

200 g jasmine rice, steamed

To prepare the red curry paste, combine all ingredients together in a deep heavy-bottomed saucepan and blend to a fine paste (or pound in a mortar and pestle). Note: use fresh herbs and spices where possible and use within two days of preparation. To prepare crab dish, heat red curry paste and add coconut milk. When aromas are at their height, add chicken stock and simmer. Just before serving, add palm sugar, fish sauce and lime leaves then add lime juice to give required sharpness. To serve, heat sauce and crab pieces and bok choy. Cook until crab is red, approximately 5-7 minutes. Serve garnished with coriander and sliced red chilli and accompany with jasmine rice.

Serves 4.

No.44 King Street, Perth, Western Australia.

Left: Fremantle. The largest port in the State and a bustling city, 19 kilometres south of Perth.

Right: Nullarbor Plain — 20 million years ago, this, the largest single slab of limestone in the world, was pushed upward from under the sea to form a plateau covering 200,000 square kilometres.

Inset: Traffic is never a problem on the Nullarbor — but pedestrians can be (see below).

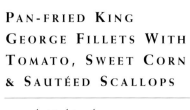

PAN-FRIED KING GEORGE FILLETS WITH TOMATO, SWEET CORN & SAUTÉED SCALLOPS

50 g chopped parsley
grated rind of 2 lemons
2 cloves garlic, crushed
2 whole King George whiting, filleted
with skin on
2 tomatoes, blanched and sliced
1 cob sweetcorn
6 local scallops, muscle removed
lemon olive oil
basil oil

Chop parsley, add lemon rind and garlic, and mix together. Coat the fillets on skin side. Seal fillets in pan then oven bake for 3-5 minutes. Sauté tomato and sweetcorn, add seared scallops. Place fillets on top of tomato and scallops, dress with lemon olive oil and a drizzle of basil oil. Serves 2.

FRASER'S RESTAURANT, WEST PERTH, WESTERN AUSTRALIA.

Below: Estimated to be 3000 million years old, the awesome 25 metre high Wave Rock at Hyden has been naturally sculpted out of granite.

COCONUT PRAWNS WITH SPICED MANGO CHUTNEY

MANGO CHUTNEY

2 ripe mangoes, flesh only

1/4 cup firmly packed brown sugar

1 clove garlic

1/2 medium red onion

1/2 red chilli

6 peppercorns

2 cloves

1 cinnamon stick

1/4 cup each sultanas, white wine vinegar

pinch salt

1/2 teaspoon each ground allspice,
ground ginger

PRAWNS

1 egg

100 ml coconut milk

salt and pepper

flour

16 x U15 (large) cleaned tiger prawns

shredded coconut

vegetable oil

To make the mango chutney, combine all ingredients and leave to stand overnight. Simmer for 20 minutes over gentle heat. Cool before use. Makes 300 g. To prepare the prawns, make an eggwash with egg, coconut milk, salt and pepper. Lightly flour prawns and dust off excess. Dip in eggwash and drain excess off. Roll in shredded coconut. Fry prawns in fresh hot vegetable oil until golden. Drain. Serve over mango chutney. Serves 4.

JESSICA'S SEAFOOD RESTAURANT, PERTH, WESTERN AUSTRALIA.

CHICKEN RAMEN

RAMEN SOUP STOCK
6 chicken carcasses
1 each small onion, small carrot,
celery stick
Chinese leaves, dried
peppercorns
bay leaves

2 x 120 g chicken breasts
350 ml Ramen soup stock
125 g noodles
2 small bok choy
GARNISH
4 medium oyster mushrooms
1 chilli
enoki mushrooms

To prepare the stock, place the bones and all the ingredients in a pot, cover with water and bring to the boil. Simmer the stock for at least two hours, skimming the surface regularly. After two hours strain through a fine sieve. To prepare the chicken, grill chicken breasts until cooked through. Heat the soup stock with the noodles, bring to the boil and add the bok choy and simmer for two minutes. Place the noodles on the bottom of the bowl. Slice the chicken breasts on an angle and then arrange the sliced chicken, bok choy and oyster mushrooms around the edge. Carefully pour the chicken stock over and garnish with the chilli and enoki mushrooms.
Serves 2.

COCO'S, SOUTH PERTH,
WESTERN AUSTRALIA.

UNCONQUERED

With the exception of the extreme south-west and north-east corners, Western Australia is desert. Running through the centre of the state, the Gibson Desert (pictured) steadfastly resists all human intrusions. This is the 'dead' interior. A scorching, desolate place with endless, open spinifex plains and sand ridges marching to the horizon for hundreds of kilometres.

But even in this wilderness, there is enough occasional rain to sustain a unique variety of animals and plants.

PORK IN BBQ SAUCE

SAUCE

2 tablespoons each oil, sugar

4 tablespoons HP sauce

1 teaspoon each salt, chilli sauce

1 tablespoon oyster sauce

3 tablespoons tomato sauce

½ cup water

300 g pork loin chops

2 tablespoons oil

1 lettuce leaf

1 small onion, sliced

To make the sauce, combine all ingredients. Heat the oil in wok, add pork and stir-fry until cooked. Pour oil and pork through strainer, setting aside separately. Pour sauce ingredients and pork into wok and heat through. Garnish with lettuce and onion.

Serves 1.

JOE'S ORIENTAL DINER,
HYATT REGENCY, PERTH,
WESTERN AUSTRALIA.

Left: Moonrise over the Bungle Bungle Range, one of the most remarkable natural features in Australia, covering some 640 square kilometres of the Ord River Valley.

STIR-FRIED SEAFOOD WITH GINGER & OYSTER SAUCE

SAUCE

¼ teaspoon chopped garlic

2 teaspoons each oyster sauce, soy sauce

1 teaspoon sugar

¼ teaspoon salt

⅛ teaspoon white pepper

2 tablespoons oil

¼ teaspoon sesame oil

100 ml chicken stock

2 teaspoons cornflour

1–2 tablespoons oil

50 g each prawns, scallops, squid

1 tablespoon each onion, green capsicum,
red capsicum, baby corn, bamboo shoots

To make the sauce, mix all ingredients except cornflour and bring to the boil. Combine cornflour with water and stir into sauce, cooking until thick. Heat the oil in wok. Place seafood into hot oil and stir-fry for about 2-3 minutes. Pour oil and seafood through strainer, setting aside separately. Add a little oil to wok, cook onion, capsicum, corn and bamboo shoots. Place seafood back into wok with sauce mixture and boil until sauce has thickened.
Serves 1-2.

JOE'S ORIENTAL DINER,
HYATT REGENCY, PERTH,
WESTERN AUSTRALIA.

The Great Sandy Desert. Covering an area the size of Great Britain & Italy, this boundless sea of sand stretches from the Northern Territory border to the Indian Ocean, south of Broome.

CABLE BEACH'S MARINATED PEARL MEAT

Two marinades are provided — each will provide enough to marinate 500 g thinly sliced pearl meat

GINGER & SOY MARINADE

4 cloves garlic, julienned
2 tablespoons chopped chives
1 red chilli, julienned
4 slices fresh root ginger, julienned
1 tablespoon each salt, sesame oil
2 tablespoons each sugar, soy sauce,
white wine
3 tablespoons each ketchup, white wine
vinegar

Place the pearl meat in a bowl. Combine all other ingredients. Pour over the meat, cover and refrigerate for several hours. The meat will take on a 'cooked' appearance. Can be served with a salad. Serves 5-6 as a starter.

PINK PEPPERCORN & MUSTARD SEED MARINADE

125 ml olive oil
¼ cup fresh lime juice
2 tablespoons pink peppercorns
1 tablespoon grain mustard
⅛ bunch finely chopped coriander

Place the pearl meat in a bowl. Combine all other ingredients. Pour over the meat, cover and refrigerate for several hours. The meat will take on a 'cooked' appearance. Can be served with a salad. Serves 5-6 as a starter.

CABLE BEACH INTER-CONTINENTAL RESORT, BROOME, WESTERN AUSTRALIA.

PEARL OF THE WEST

Cable Beach (above & right) was so named when the underwater communications link was established between Broome and Java in the 19th century. Once the world's pearling capital, with a population of 5000, and a fleet of 400 luggers crowding the port, Broome reached its peak in the 1920s. However, the industry went into slow decline. Eventually, a growing tourist industry became a major influence in preventing Broome from becoming a ghost town.

Closer to Bali than to Perth, and with an international airport, Broome is lively and cosmopolitan. There are plenty of activities — bush safaris, scenic flights, skydiving, cruises to the coral reefs. And of course there is the 22 kilometre Cable Beach — ideal for a day relaxing in the sun or a sunset camel ride.

NORTHERN TERRITORY

LIKE THE MAGNIFICENT KATA TJUTA (the Olgas) and the world's biggest monolith, Uluru (Ayers Rock) — shown here — everything in the Northern Territory is larger than life. From the arid Red Centre in the south to the monsoonal Top End, this is big-sky country where nature predominates. Here, you will experience a very different Australia.

Despite its vastness — an area eight times the size of Great Britain with only 1 percent of the Australian population — the Northern Territory fits comfortably into a travel itinerary. Alice Springs — 'the Alice' as it's usually known — is the natural base for exploring the Red Centre, an untamed, sometimes surreal world of scorching deserts, eerie gorges, meteorite craters, and the wonders of Uluru and Kata Tjuta. This is an ancient world that has inspired many legends of the Dreamtime. At the other end of the 'the Track' — the 1500 kilometre Sturt Highway which has an amazing variety of interesting places along the way — is the Top End and Darwin, capital of the Northern Territory. Warm weather, excellent beaches and a cosmopolitan atmosphere make this tropical city an ideal base for your exploration of the wild and fascinating country at the Top End.

PRAWN, MANGO & WILD LIME TIMBALE SALAD

50 prawns, cooked

5 mangoes

100 g wild limes

100 ml mayonnaise

DRESSING

20 passionfruit

100 ml olive oil

50 ml lemon juice

5 heads baby cos lettuce

5 lemons for wedges

red capsicum, julienned, for garnish

Dice prawns, mangoes and wild limes into 1 cm x 1 cm cubes. Bind with mayonnaise and put in timbale moulds and refrigerate.

To make dressing, combine passionfruit pulp, olive oil and lemon juice. Wash lettuce and place on plate. Place timbales on top and drizzle with dressing. Garnish with lemon wedges and red capsicum. Serves 10.

CORNUCOPIA MUSEUM CAFÉ, FANNIE BAY, NORTHERN TERRITORY.

Left: The Museum and Art Gallery of the Northern Territory.
Above left: Parliament House.

ADVENTUROUS TUCKER

If you have a taste for the exotic, you'll relish the Northern Territory eating scene. Here 'bush tucker' is regarded as 'gourmet' food. Native Australian dishes include Char-grilled Kangaroo with a Roasted Mushroom and Hunter Sauce; Lemon-grass-scented Baby Silver Barramundi; together with crocodile, water buffalo, emu, camel and magpie geese, golden snapper, Spanish mackerel, pearl meat and mud crabs.

Darwin, one of Australia's most multicultural cities, is also a showcase for ethnic cuisine. For the best all-round eating experience in Darwin, join the crowds that gather at the Mindil Beach markets every Thursday evening during the dry season. Here, you can watch the sun go down over the Timor Sea as you enjoy your choice of Brazilian, Filipino, Indian, Laotian, Greek, German, Indonesian, Slovak, Turkish, Sri Lankan, Chinese, Malaysian or Portuguese cuisine.

For those with an adventurous appetite, those who like a touch of the exotic in their tucker, the Northern Territory offers some interesting culinary challenges.

CHAR-GRILLED KANGAROO SERVED WITH A ROASTED MUSHROOM & HUNTER SAUCE

SAUCE

6 rashers bacon, julienned
30 whole button mushrooms, roasted
1 Spanish onion, finely diced
1 teaspoon crushed garlic
1 punnet of cherry tomatoes, halved
½ bunch rosemary
600 ml jus (reduced beef stock)

30 potatoes
butter
3 kg kangaroo, cut into 300 g portions
10 large mushrooms, roasted

To prepare the sauce, lightly sauté bacon, mushrooms, onion and garlic. Add cherry tomatoes and rosemary to the jus. Par-cook potatoes in boiling water then fried in butter. To assemble, place large mushrooms in centre of plate and spread potatoes around outside of plate. Char-grill kangaroo steaks to medium rare. Place on top of mushrooms and drizzle sauce over top.
Serves 10.

CORNUCOPIA MUSEUM CAFÉ, FANNIE BAY, NORTHERN TERRITORY.

LEMON-GRASS-SCENTED BABY SILVER BARRAMUNDI

DRESSING

4 cloves garlic
2 tablespoons grated ginger
2 red chillies, seeded
1/2 cup each palm sugar, lime juice,
fish sauce
1 cup water

FISH

6 plate-size baby barramundi
6 stems lemon grass, split lengthwise but
joined at root end

GARNISH

6 stems hot Vietnamese mint

GREEN PAPAYA SALAD

1 green papaya, skin removed, grated
2 cloves fresh garlic, minced
1/2 cup each palm sugar, coconut vinegar
1 medium chilli, minced
1/2 cup roasted, chopped peanuts
1/2 bunch coriander leaves and root,
chopped
1/2 cup fresh lime or lemon juice

TURMERIC RICE

2 cups long grain rice
2 cups coconut milk
1 teaspoon turmeric powder
1 bay leaf
1 cinnamon stick
3 cracked cardamom pods

DREAMTIME TERRITORY

Kakadu National Park (pictured) has been widely acclaimed as the 'jewel in the Top End crown'. An easy three hour drive east of Darwin, this outstanding World Heritage wilderness area is one of the natural marvels of Australia. Covering over 20,000 square kilometres, the country's largest national park is a spectacular kaleidoscope of superb landscapes, teeming wildlife and some of Australia's best Aboriginal rock art.

A 300 kilometre drive south down 'the Track' from Darwin will bring you to the crossroads of the Top End and the bustling town of Katherine, the Territory's third largest centre. Just 30 kilometres to the north-east lies

To prepare the dressing, crush garlic, ginger, chilli and palm sugar with mortar and pestle, add lime juice. Add fish sauce and water a little at a time, testing until desired flavour is reached. To prepare the fish, scale and gut barramundi. Make three shallow cuts on each side. Tie split lemon grass at head of fish with a loose knot. Bring tail towards head and tie in place. Place in steamer, cook until flesh is white and just starting to come away from the bones. Spoon the dressing over cooked fish and garnish with mint. Serve with turmeric rice and green papaya salad. To prepare the green papaya salad, mix the ingredients in a large bowl then crush and squeeze with hands to blend the flavours. (The salad will keep for up to a week if refrigerated.)

To prepare turmeric rice, rinse the rice and soak for 1 hour. Drain and place in a heavy-bottomed saucepan with all other ingredients. Boil until the liquid is absorbed. Remove the bay leaf, cardamom pods and cinnamon stick. Stir. Cover, cook a further 10 minutes on a very low heat. Transfer to serving bowls. Serves 6.

LINDSAY STREET CAFÉ, DARWIN, NORTHERN TERRITORY.

the famous Nitmiluk (Katherine Gorge) National Park. Strictly speaking, this fascinating river canyon is 13 gorges, separated from each other by rapids. You can view the abundant wildlife and larger-than-life Aboriginal paintings from a walking track, canoe or tour boat.

Best-known of all the wilderness reserves in the stunning Red Centre is the vast, World Heritage listed, Uluru-Kata Tjuta National Park, 460 kilometres south-west of Alice Springs. Rising above a vast, sandy spinifex plain the world-renowned Uluru (Ayers Rock) and the equally impressive but less well-known Kata Tjuta (the Olgas) will overwhelm you. Photo top right shows Aboriginal Rock Art at Kakadu National Park. Here, at the heart of the world's oldest continent, everything is larger than life.

PLUMP ROAST QUAIL ON POLENTA

1 tablespoon each butter, finely chopped
chives, finely chopped prosciutto
¼ cup Arborio rice
approximately 1 litre hot chicken stock
¼ cup polenta
4 quail, deboned
4 rashers bacon
1 tablespoon olive oil
¼ clove garlic, finely chopped
10 rosemary leaves
4 sage leaves

Place butter, chives, prosciutto and rice into a deep frypan and lightly sauté for 1 minute. Slowly add 2 cups chicken stock a little at a time until rice is cooked. Cool. Bring remaining chicken stock to the boil in a pot. Slowly add polenta, stirring constantly for 5 minutes until thick. Remove mixture from the pot and place on a well-oiled worktop and roll to about 3 cm thick then cut into slabs. Place quail, breast side up, in a non-stick ovenproof dish. Place the rice mixture evenly into the cavity of each quail and close up, locking the wings together. Tightly wrap with bacon and secure with a toothpick.

Place olive oil, garlic, rosemary and sage over the quail. Bake in a hot oven for 20 minutes. Warm the polenta slabs under the grill or in the oven. Place the quails on top of polenta then baste the quails with oil from the baking tray. Garnish with the rosemary and sage leaves.

Serves 2.

RISTORANTE PUCCINI, ALICE SPRINGS, NORTHERN TERRITORY.

Above: Alice Springs. Lying at the heart of the Red Centre, this sun-scorched town is 1500 kilometres from the nearest capital city.

Left: The world-famous Uluru (Ayers Rock) is nine kilometres in circumference and rises a towering 348 metres above the surrounding plain.

QUEENSLAND

BIG, SUNNY QUEENSLAND is Australia's holiday state. It's where the rest of the country would rather be when winter arrives. Almost the size of western Europe, Australia's second-largest state is also big on contrasts and surprises.

You can luxuriate in the glitz, glamour and good life of the Gold Coast. Or pit yourself against the wilderness of Cape York Peninsula — the last frontier. You can enjoy the pleasures of a nine hour gourmet tour of the Sunshine Coast. Or take the wheel of a 4WD to explore Fraser Island — the world's largest sand island. You can sip Chablis and watch a cane toad race on a balmy tropical night in Port Douglas. Or quaff a beer and shout yourself hoarse in the burning outback sun at the Birdsville Picnic Races. You can tour the wineries of the Granite Belt. Or test yourself game-fishing off Cairns. You can fossick in the heat and dust of the southern hemisphere's largest sapphire fields near Emerald. Or lose yourself in the wonders of the world's oldest tropical rainforest in the lush, wildly and spectacularly beautiful Far North. And, of course, Queensland has Australia's number one attraction — the Great Barrier Reef (pictured).

PAN-FRIED HERVEY BAY SCALLOPS ON A TIAN OF ROASTED CONTINENTAL EGGPLANT WITH CARAMELISED CAPSICUM AND AGED BALSAMIC COMPOTE

AGED BALSAMIC DRESSING
1 tablespoon 20 year old balsamic vinegar
1 teaspoon lemon juice
2 tablespoons grapeseed oil
½ teaspoon Dijon mustard
TIAN OF ROASTED CONTINENTAL EGGPLANT
2 eggplants
1 ripe tomato
1 clove garlic
sprig of thyme

½ each yellow, green and red capsicums
16 (size U8) scallops
GARNISH
deep-fried parsnip

To prepare the dressing, thoroughly blend all ingredients. Cut eggplant into 4 cm lengths and char-grill. Wrap in tinfoil with a slice of tomato, garlic and thyme and bake until soft. Remove from foil and place in the centre of the plate. Roast capsicum halves and peel. Cut into 5 mm dice. Place around eggplant tian. Pan-fry scallops and place four per serve on top of the eggplant. Drizzle with aged balsamic dressing and garnish with deep-fried parsnip.
Serves 4.

SIGGI'S, THE HERITAGE HOTEL, BRISBANE, QUEENSLAND.

COAST WITH A BOAST

Only an hour's drive south of Brisbane, the Gold Coast styles itself as the nation's tourist capital. With nearly 300 days of sunshine each year and over 40 kilometres of beaches stretching from Southport in the north to Coolangatta in the south, it's a magnet that attracts over three

million visitors annually. The permanent population, already well over 180,000, is growing at seven per cent a year, or four times the national average.

The Gold Coast caters for all tastes. You can go fishing, boating, scuba diving, surfing, water-skiing and hot-air ballooning. Or you can enjoy some of Australia's best bushwalking in the magnificent subtropical hinterland. The Gold Coast also boasts some of the country's major theme parks including Seaworld, the largest marine park in the southern hemisphere; Dreamworld; Wet 'n' Wild, Australia's largest aquatic park; and Movie World, the only Hollywood theme park in the southern hemisphere.

And, as you might expect, the Gold Coast claims more restaurants per square kilometre than any other Australian city.

RARE PEPPERED SALMON

GINGER LIME VINAIGRETTE

3 tablespoons soy sauce
juice of 2 limes
1 teaspoon minced fresh ginger
salt
freshly ground white pepper
4 tablespoons extra virgin olive oil

SALMON

1 tablespoon olive oil
4 x 80 g pieces salmon
ground black pepper and sea salt
1 small avocado, diced
4 teaspoons trout roe
4 teaspoons finely diced red onion
4 sprigs watercress

To make the vinaigrette, place all ingredients except olive oil into a food processor on high speed. Slowly add oil as one would for a mayonnaise. To prepare the salmon, heat oil in a heavy pan over high heat. Roll the salmon in pepper and sea salt mix, sear salmon on all sides, approximately 10 seconds per side.

Do not allow to rest. Cover plate with dressing. In the centre place one quarter of the avocado. Slice salmon lengthways and place on top of avocado. Place half a teaspoon of roe and half a teaspoon of onion around the salmon. Garnish with watercress and serve immediately.

Serves 4.

INDIGO BAR BISTRO, NEW FARM, QUEENSLAND.

Above: A monument to success. The Gold Coast skyline.

Below: The Corkscrew at Seaworld, the largest marine theme park in the southern hemisphere.

RELAXED TASTES

Brisbane, Australia's third-largest city and home to nearly half of Queensland's population, emerged from dark beginnings. Like Sydney and Hobart, this sunny capital began as a penal settlement. Today, Brisbane is a cosmopolitan city with the atmosphere of a friendly country town. The easygoing lifestyle is dictated by the subtropical setting. When you live in a city that has a year-round average of $7^1/_2$ hours of sunshine a day, endless balmy evenings and a winter when it is just cool enough to wear a sweater, life is more laid back. The fast pace of the capitals south of the border is best kept where it belongs.

In recent years, Brisbane's restaurant and café scene has blossomed — Rare Peppered Salmon; Caramelised Banana Pizza & Honey Gelato; Grilled Snapper Fillet, Sweet & Sour Vegetables, Rocket & Citrus Aioli; Pan-fried Hervey Bay Scallops with Roasted Continental Eggplant, Caramelised Capsicum and Aged Balsamic Compote — are just a taste of the treats you can now savour.

At the north-eastern end of the city, fronting the Brisbane River, you will find two of the best and most popular food complexes. The Eagle St Pier features impressive Italian cuisine and sophisticated Queensland seafood dishes. Award-winning classical cuisine, with an emphasis on

STEAMED CHINESE GREENS WITH OYSTER SAUCE

300 g green vegetables (kai lan)
1 tablespoon oil
½ teaspoon chopped garlic
3 tablespoons oyster sauce
1 tablespoon chicken broth
1 teaspoon each rice wine, potato starch
½ red chilli flower
1 shallot flower

Cook vegetables in boiling water for 1 minute then cut into 8 cm long pieces and arrange on the centre of the plate. Heat wok and add oil, garlic, oyster sauce, chicken broth and rice wine. Thicken with potato starch. Put on top of vegetables. Garnish with chilli and shallot flower and serve while hot.
Serves 1.

ZEN BAR, BRISBANE CITY, QUEENSLAND.

local seafood, is a feature of the Riverside Centre. Fortitude Valley and New Farm are definitely gourmet territory. Here, you can enjoy the best that Queensland has to offer — everything from mud crab ravioli through to kangaroo steaks. You also have a choice of Chinese, Vietnamese, Korean, Italian and French restaurants.

Brisbane's culinary climate is ideal for gourmets.

PRESSED TERRINE OF SMOKED TOMATOES ON AN AVOCADO RATATOUILLE & WARM GYMPIE FARM GOATS' CHEESE

TOMATO TERRINE

1.5 kg whole tomatoes

1 large bunch basil, washed

750 ml olive oil

200 g each garlic, shallots, sliced

300 ml balsamic vinegar

salt and pepper

RATATOUILLE

1 small zucchini, blanched

1 red capsicum, roasted and skinned

1 red onion

8 olives, pitted

juice of 1 lime

2 avocados

juice of 1 lemon

¼ bunch each coriander, Italian parsley, basil, sliced

Gympie Farm goats' cheese

To prepare the terrine, firstly make tomato leaves by peeling tomatoes and smoking the skins and cutting into petals or leaves. Make a marinade by mixing 3/4 of the basil and all other ingredients except the tomato leaves. Place tomatoes in a bowl and pour the marinade over them. Leave to marinate overnight. Line a terrine with plastic film. Season the inside of the terrine. Place 3 or 4 basil leaves on the bottom. Place the drained tomato leaves tightly in a layer then season, place a couple of basil leaves. Repeat this process until the tomato layers are above the edges of the terrine. Cover with plastic film. Place in a cool room and press with a weight for at least 24 hours. To make the ratatouille, finely dice the zucchini, capsicum, onion and olives and sauté for about 5 minutes. Mix in the lime juice. Dice the avocado slightly bigger and place in water and lemon juice to prevent discolouring. Drain avocado and combine with all other ingredients. To serve, spoon the ratatouille onto six serving plates and top with slices of terrine and goats' cheese.
Serves 6.

TABLES OF TOOWONG,
TOOWONG, QUEENSLAND.

*Left: King George Square, Brisbane.
A restful oasis in the heart of a
cosmopolitan city.*

SMOKED SALMON WITH CHILLI CORNCAKES, ROCKET & SOUSED LEEKS

CORNCAKES

100 g flour

1 cup buttermilk

¼ teaspoon baking soda

2 teaspoons baking powder

2 eggs, separated

¼ cup Italian parsley and coriander,
chopped

1 cup corn kernels, roasted

½ teaspoon finely chopped chilli

salt and freshly ground black pepper

SOUSED LEEKS

2 leeks

1 cup crème fraîche

juice and zest of 1 lemon

salt and freshly ground black pepper

DRESSING

100 ml olive oil

juice of 1 lemon

1 teaspoon coriander seeds, roasted

salt and freshly ground black pepper

1 tablespoon chopped chives

1 tomato, peeled, seeded and diced

SALAD

8 slices smoked salmon

rocket

tomatoes, oven roasted

1 Spanish onion, sliced

To make the corncakes, place flour in a bowl and whisk in buttermilk, baking soda, baking powder and egg yolks. Fold in chopped herbs, roasted corn and chilli. Add whipped egg whites and seasonings. Cook heaped spoonfuls in a buttered frying pan or in moulds in the oven. To prepare the leeks, wash thoroughly and slice. Sweat over heat until transparent in colour. Cool leeks well.

Add remaining souse ingredients. To make the dressing, whisk oil, lemon juice, coriander seeds and salt and pepper. Fold in chives and tomato. To assemble, place a warm corncake in the centre of each serving plate. Top each corncake with 1 spoon of soused leeks. Twist 1 slice of smoked salmon on top. Combine rocket, dressing, tomatoes, onion and arrange on top of salmon. Add a second twisted slice of salmon then drizzle dressing over salmon and around edges of plate. Season with freshly ground black pepper and serve immediately.

Serves 4.

E'CCO LICENSED BISTRO, BRISBANE, QUEENSLAND.

Above: One of Brisbane's many colourful shopping malls.

MIRACLE SANDS

If you enjoy sailing, surfing, fishing, walking and space to yourself, Fraser Island is the ideal holiday destination. Fraser (pictured) is the world's largest sand island — 123 kilometres long by 15 kilometres wide and rising in places to 200 metres — and was added to the World Heritage list in 1992. Sparsely populated, with a few small holiday

CARAMELISED BANANA PIZZA & HONEY GELATO

CRÈME ANGLAISE

2¹/₂ cups cream

5 egg yolks

³/₄ cup sugar

Heat cream to almost boiling, whisk yolks and sugar to ribbon. Add cream and whisk until smooth, place on low flame and stir with wooden spoon until thick enough to coat spoon, do not boil.

HONEY GELATO

2 cups milk

6 egg yolks

1¹/₂ cups cream

250 g Leatherwood honey

Bring milk to boil. Whisk yolks and cream, add honey and whisk in boiled milk. Allow to cool. Churn in an ice-cream maker or food processor. Freeze.

BANANA PIZZA

4 x puff pastry discs (approximately 10 cm in diameter)

egg yolk

3 large ripe bananas

100 g castor sugar

Dot pastry with a fork and glaze with egg yolk. Bake in 250°C oven until golden brown. Allow to cool. Peel and slice bananas diagonally and fan over the top of pastry. Sprinkle with castor sugar and burn with a blow torch until caramelised. Serve with Crème Anglaise and Honey Gelato. Serves 4.

IL CENTRO RESTAURANT & BAR, BRISBANE, QUEENSLAND.

centres, the island is 4WD country — there are no sealed roads. And despite an annual influx of over 20,000 vehicles, it remains wild and unspoiled. There are superb beaches; remote dunes that offer a real challenge to 4WD and beach buggy explorers; vast expanses of dripping rainforest and over 40 freshwater lakes, some of them superb for swimming.

Fraser Island is a rarity. A World Heritage site that is totally accessible to the public.

MUD CRAB OMELET

¼ cup each beansprouts, chopped corn,
bamboo shoots, julienned carrot
12 leaves tat soi
1-2 tablespoons oil

THAI PRAWN DRESSING

1 teaspoon each Tom Yum paste, nam
prik pao
½ teaspoon sambal oeleck
2 tablespoons ketjap manis
½ cup palm sugar
juice of 1 lime
1 clove garlic, crushed
100 ml water

12 eggs
salt and pepper
200 g mud crab meat

Stir-fry vegetables and divide onto
plates. Combine all ingredients for
the dressing and spoon some onto
each plate. Make four omelets and
place crab meat inside. Fold over
and slide onto plates. Garnish with
coriander leaves.

Serves 4.

TWO SMALL ROOMS, TOOWONG,
QUEENSLAND.

A WORLD OF WONDER

Guarding the eastern coast of Queensland is one of the natural wonders of the world — the Great Barrier Reef (pictured) — stretching for over 2300 kilometres from the Gulf of Papua in the north to Bundaberg in the south. The Reef is a living phenomenon comprised of layer after layer of polyps — tiny, rapidly reproducing marine invertebrates which secrete limestone. There are more than 340 varieties of coral with the myriad colours being determined by the state of decay. Made up of over 2500 separate, inter-connected reefs covering 230,000 square kilometres, the Great Barrier Reef is the largest living thing on earth. So large in fact that, in 1770, James Cook sailed for 1000 kilometres inside the Reef before suspecting its existence.

Protected as a significant World Heritage site and, as the world's largest marine park, the Great Barrier Reef is Australia's number one attraction.

GRILLED SNAPPER FILLET, SWEET & SOUR VEGETABLES, ROCKET & CITRUS AIOLI

(FILETTI DI PESCE CON INSALATA DI CAPONATA AGLA DOLCE)

1 cup each brown sugar, white wine vinegar
1 eggplant, diced
4 zucchini, diced
2 red capsicum, diced
1 brown onion, diced
4 egg tomatoes, diced
100 ml olive oil
1 clove garlic
200 ml pelati (peeled tomatoes)

4 x 200 g snapper fillets
GARNISH
rocket leaves
garlic mayonnaise
seasoning

Boil sugar and vinegar and pour over diced vegetables. Allow to cool. Strain liquid from vegetables and reserve. Sauté vegetables in large pot with olive oil and garlic. Add peeled tomatoes and 1 cup of reserved liquid. Reduce by half. Grill fish fillets. Place sweet and sour vegetables on plates with several rocket leaves on top, place grilled fish on top of this, finish with a dollop of garlic mayonnaise and season. Serves 4.

IL CENTRO RESTAURANT & BAR, BRISBANE, QUEENSLAND.

The Great Barrier Reef has fish in an
estimated 1500 variations of shape, colour
and size.

GRILLED SARDINES ON WOK-TOSSED GREENS WITH CASHEW NUT & CAPSICUM SALSA

Use fresh sardines (ours come from Western Australia). They are deheaded and butterflied, with the centre bone removed. Have salad greens and other ingredients ready.

8 fresh sardines
200 ml basil-infused light olive oil
100 ml rice wine

Brush sardines with basil oil and cook lightly and quickly on medium-high. Do not overheat. Remove and deglaze pan with 100 ml rice wine and 50 ml basil oil. Mix well, season if needed, then toss salad greens quickly. Do not overheat. Serve with the salsa.

CASHEW NUT SALSA

200 ml light virgin olive oil
50 ml each balsamic vinegar, white wine
salt and pepper
100 g cashew nuts, roughly chopped and lightly toasted
2 shallots, finely chopped
1/2 medium capsicum, seeded and finely chopped
2 teaspoons finely chopped Italian parsley
6 green olives, pitted and chopped

To make salsa, mix together olive oil, vinegar, white wine and seasoning. Add other ingredients and mix well.
Serves 4.

FISHLIPS BAR & GRILL, CAIRNS, QUEENSLAND.

ISLAND ESCAPES

The Whitsundays (pictured) are probably Queensland's best-known islands. Named by Captain Cook, who sailed through on Whit Sunday 1770, these magnificent islands were designated national parks by forward-thinking governments in the 1930s and 1940s, and even today most are uninhabited with tourism being carefully controlled. Camping is permitted on a number of the 74 islands and there are developed holiday resorts on seven. Brampton Island — the closest to Mackay, is mostly national park. Activities include exploring the snorkelling trail (with a waterproof map). Lindeman Island — the resort here is Australia's first

Club Med. Hamilton Island — the most developed of the islands with a small town and port and a jet airstrip with non-stop flights to major cities. Offering a seemingly limitless range of activities, this is not the place for a quiet island sojourn. Long Island — an idyllic getaway for those who like solitude. Three small, unpretentious resorts offer all you need to fulfil a tropical holiday dream. South Molle Island — a mecca for families with children being well catered for. Daydream Island — tiny, jewel-like and close to the mainland, this was one of the first islands to welcome guests in the 1930s. Today, it is a popular family resort. Hayman Island — synonymous with the idea of a Barrier Reef holiday and a big favourite with honeymooners — is a five-star resort.

SMOKED SALMON LAYER CAKE WITH HORSERADISH CREAM

2 eggplants
Cajun seasoning or paprika powder
olive oil
250 g cream cheese
juice of 1 lemon
pinch each salt, white pepper
HORSERADISH CREAM
100 ml cream
1-2 tablespoons freshly grated horseradish
whipped cream

3 sheets dried seaweed (nori)
250 g smoked salmon

Cut eggplant into thin slices. Sprinkle with Cajun mix and fry in olive oil until soft. Remove from heat and leave to cool. Mix cream cheese with lemon juice, salt and pepper. Stir until soft. To make horseradish cream, whip cream until stiff peaks form. Gently fold into horseradish. Layer eggplant, seaweed, cream cheese and salmon — repeat. Refrigerate for a few hours before serving. Serve with horseradish cream and crisp bread such as lavash or grissini sticks. Serves 4.

CAIRNS GAME FISHING CLUB,
CAIRNS, QUEENSLAND.

FRUITS OF DISCOVERY

Queensland's sugar industry (right and below) has always been highly organised and prosperous. Sugar cane is grown on small privately owned farms along the coastal belt and sugar production exceeds Australia's needs. The surplus is exported.

Rich, fertile soils, warm temperatures, together with abundant sunshine and rainfall, create ideal growing conditions for exotic, tropical fruits. Bananas and pineapples are produced in small holdings in the hills and ranges north and south of Brisbane. Other exotics include mangoes, rambutan, avocados, custard apples, figs, nashi and papaya. Nuts such as pecans, peanuts, macadamias and almonds grow in coastal plantations and citrus fruits in the south-east of the state. The success of this pot-pourri of fruits has led to a substantial fruit-canning and jam-making industry in Queensland.

Tropical fruits, together with diverse local seafoods including mud crabs (muddies), Moreton Bay Bugs, tiger prawns and an abundance of reef fish — Coral Trout, King Snapper, Red Emperor, Scarlet Sea Perch, Parrot Fish, Sweet Lip and Hussar — provide eating experiences that are distinctively Queensland.

SEAFOOD MOSAIQUE

1 each swede, turnip, large carrot

½ leek

1 cup sauterne or sweet white wine

125 g butter

12 each green Morton Bay bugs, peeled

green prawns, scallops, baby octopus

4 x 80 g tuna steaks

2 teaspoons olive oil

pinch salt

Peel the swede, turnip and carrot and cut into fine ribbons. Cut leek in rounds. Wash carefully and keep separate. Bring sauterne and butter to boil. Add carrot, turnip, swede, bugmeat and prawns. Simmer for approximately 3 minutes then add scallops and octopus and finally the leeks. Cook for 1 minute. At the same time sear the tuna steaks in a hot pan with olive oil, approximately 1 minute each side. Season. Serve with shellfish and vegetables. This dish is best served with rice.

Serves 4.

CAIRNS GAME FISHING CLUB,
CAIRNS, QUEENSLAND.

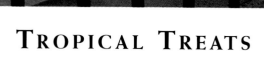

TROPICAL TREATS

Cairns, dubbed 'the gateway to paradise', is the capital of the tropical Far North. Until the 1980s, this colourful coastal city was a sleepy backwater. Nothing had changed much in the century since it was founded. Now, Cairns is firmly established as one of Australia's top tourist destinations, boasting an international airport, bustling shopping malls and restaurants offering cuisine from around the globe with menus posted in English, German and Japanese. As our featured dishes indicate, innovative Aussie bush tucker — Sautéed Crocodile Strips on Sweet Potato & Red

*Left: A tropical view from the Cairns
Game Fishing Club. The waters of the region
are world-famous for game fishing.
Inset: The Cairns Casino.*

Curry Fritters; Emu Fan Fillet with Emu Wonton; Sweet Potato Mash &
Native Aniseed Butter Sauce; Lemon Myrtle Bavarois with Rosella Flower
Jelly — are firm favourites.

Cairns' location is superb. The Great Barrier Reef to the east, the
mountain rainforests and lush Atherton Tablelands to the west, and white,
palm-fringed beaches to the north and south. And whatever activity
you're interested in, you'll find it here — not only easy access to the Great
Barrier Reef for snorkelling, scuba diving and game fishing but white-
water rafting, canoeing, horse riding, bungy jumping and sky diving.

Cairns is the gateway to good times.

SAUTÉED CROCODILE STRIPS ON SWEET POTATO & RED CURRY FRITTERS WITH PARSLEY & PECAN NUT SALSA

SWEET POTATO FRITTERS

300 g sweet potato, peeled
1 small onion
oil for frying
1 teaspoon minced garlic
1 teaspoon Thai red curry paste
¼ cup each plain flour,
self-raising flour
salt and pepper
1 egg, beaten

Cook sweet potatoes until soft but not waterlogged. Sauté onion lightly, add garlic and red curry paste and cook for 3-5 minutes, add to mashed potato, stir in, then fold in flour, salt and pepper and egg. Rest for 30 minutes, mould into dessertspoon-size and fry for approximately 3 minutes or until cooked. Centre should be soft but not gooey.

PECAN NUT SALSA

150-200 g pecan nuts
½ medium red onion, finely diced
1 medium red tomato, skinned
1 tablespoon finely chopped parsley
½ teaspoon minced garlic
150 ml olive oil
50 ml each balsamic vinegar, white wine
salt and pepper

4 x 80 g crocodile tail fillets,
thinly sliced
flour
oil

Blend pecan nuts, add onion, tomato, parsley and garlic. Beat together oil, balsamic vinegar and seasoning and mix through nut mixture. If too thick, add a little rice wine vinegar or Pinot Chardonnay. To prepare the crocodile, season sliced meat lightly as the flavour is easily compromised, then dust lightly in flour and sauté in a small amount of vegetable oil. Serve in small mounds surrounded by the fritters.
Serves 4.

FISHLIPS BAR & GRILL,
CAIRNS, QUEENSLAND.

Left: Far North Queensland is home to the world's oldest tropical rainforest, boasting at least 100 million years of continuous growth.
Inset: The Daintree River, haven for an extraordinary variety of bird life — and salt-water crocodiles.

RACK OF LAMB 'IN VOGUE' — WITH RED CAPSICUM, LIME & STAR ANISEED JUICE

2 x 8 ribs of lamb rack, trimmed of all fat
olive oil

TAPENADE
50 g pitted whole olives
25 g each anchovies, capers, sundried
tomatoes
1 clove garlic
2 teaspoons olive oil

SAUCE
1 onion
1 red capsicum
2 teaspoons olive oil
3 tablespoons dry white wine
1 cup chicken stock or water
salt and pepper
4 x star aniseed
juice of 1 lime

Pre-heat oven to 200°C. Seal lamb racks in hot pan with a drop of olive oil until evenly brown. Put aside to cool. Using butcher's twine, make lamb racks into a crown shape. To make the tapenade, mix all ingredients in a food processor to a smooth paste. Fill the opening of the shaped lamb rack with tapenade. Bake in oven for approximately 35-40 minutes. To make the sauce, cut onion and capsicum into large chunks and sauté in olive oil until soft and add white wine and cover with stock or water. Leave on a low heat for 10 minutes, add seasoning and star aniseed. Remove from heat. Strain and discard star aniseed. Blend sauce then squeeze in lime juice and serve over lamb.
Serves 4.

CAIRNS GAME FISHING CLUB, CAIRNS, QUEENSLAND.

LEMON MYRTLE BAVAROIS WITH ROSELLA FLOWER JELLY

BAVAROIS

600 ml milk
15 lemon myrtle leaves
300 g castor sugar
8 egg yolks
8 gelatine leaves
500 ml double cream

JELLY

200 g rosella flowers, chopped
2 litres water
500 g sugar
lemon juice
30 gelatine leaves

To prepare the bavarois, bring milk, shredded leaves and sugar to a slow boil. Stand for 10 minutes. Strain onto yolks and whisk slowly over a double boiler until bavarois forms. Add soaked and squeezed gelatine leaves. Stir over ice until mixture begins to thicken then fold in the cream. To prepare the jelly, bring all ingredients to the boil, strain and add soaked and squeezed gelatine leaves. Line bavarois moulds with jelly liquid and set in refrigerator. Fill centres with bavarois mix. To serve, dip mould into hot water for 3 seconds, tap out onto plates and garnish with candied rosella flowers.
Serves 8-10.

Note: Leftover rosella jelly is great for the kids (or adults). Lemon myrtle leaves are wonderful with fish or simply infused in boiled water for a refreshing tea.

RED OCHRE GRILL, CAIRNS, QUEENSLAND.

EMU FAN FILLET WITH EMU WONTON, SWEET POTATO MASH & NATIVE ANISEED BUTTER SAUCE

MASH

2 large sweet potatoes

1 large Pontiac potato

butter and seasoning

WONTONS

100 g emu meat

100 g chicken thigh

2 teaspoons sambal oeleck

1 teaspoon each fresh chopped coriander,

minced garlic, minced ginger

1 tablespoon ketcap manis

4-8 wonton wraps depending on size

cornflour

NATIVE ANISEED BUTTER SAUCE

10 native aniseed leaves (or 2 star anise)

100 ml port wine

salt and pepper

200 ml cream

dash of Vegemite or beef stock cube

100 g unsalted butter

700 g emu fan fillet, divided in four x

150 g pieces and one x 100 g piece

To prepare mash, boil potatoes until cooked. Drain and add butter and seasoning. Mash well.

Mince or process wonton ingredients together and place a tablespoonful into the centre of wonton wrappers, brush edges with cornflour mixed to a slurry with a little water. Fold as pictured, dust with cornflour and fry to golden.

To prepare sauce, mix all ingredients together and set aside.

To prepare emu fillets, pan-fry until rare then rest in oven at 90°C. Deglaze pan with port and reduce by half. Stir in Vegemite or stock, add cream and reduce carefully by 40%. Simmer gently and stir in cold cubed butter. Adjust seasoning and strain. Serve as illustrated.

Note: Emu meat is generally free range, has a low cholesterol count and a high protein amino acid balance making it extremely healthy. Because of its low-fat content do not overcook it. Insist on fresh aged meat, the best cuts being fan and flat fillet. Serves 4.

RED OCHRE GRILL, CAIRNS, QUEENSLAND.

Pages 188-189: Lying off Port Douglas, the immensely popular Low Isles, a fine little coral cay surrounded by a lagoon and topped by an old lighthouse.

Left: The trackless wastes of the Simpson Desert stretch west from Birdsville — the most isolated town in Queensland — all the way to Alice Springs in the Red Centre.

PHOTOGRAPHIC & ILLUSTRATION CREDITS

All food photographs by Ian Baker except Kenneth Irwin: p76.

Scenic photographs:

ATC: 12-13, 30, 34, 36-37, 38-39, 39, 51, 65, 68-69, 72-73, 91, 95, 116-117, 121.

Ian Baker: endpapers, 61, 83, 166-167, 168-169, 171, 182-183, 183 (inset), 184-185.

Pauline Whimp: 11 (map).

TRANZ/Camera Press: 125, 157, 158-159, 177.

TRANZ/Photo Index: 4-5, 6-7, 8-9, 14-15, 18-19, 20-21, 24-25, 25, 28-29, 30-31, 40-41, 44-45, 48, 48-49, 52-53, 54-55, 57, 58-59, 60-61, 62, 77, 78-79, 80-81, 84, 86-87, 88-89, 93, 96-97, 98-99, 100-101, 105, 108-109, 110-111, 114-115, 118-119, 124-125, 128-129, 132-133, 133, 136-137, 138, 138 (inset), 138-139, 140, 142-143, 144-145, 147, 148, 149, 150-151, 152, 153, 156-157, 159, 160-161, 162-163, 165, 172-173, 175, 178-179, 180, 181, 185 (inset), 188-189, 190-191, 194-195.

TRANZ/Spectrum: 2-3, 65, 165.

RESTAURANT GUIDE

NEW SOUTH WALES

AREA, 29 Bay Street, Double Bay, Sydney, ph +61 (02) 9363 3656

BAYSWATER BRASSERIE, 32 Bayswater Road, Kings Cross, Sydney, NSW 2011, ph +61 (02) 9357 2177

BUON RICORDO RESTAURANT, 108 Boundary Street, Paddington, NSW 2021, ph +61 (02) 9360 6729

CICADA, 29 Challis Avenue, Potts Point, NSW 2011, ph +61 (02) 9358 1255

FORTY ONE RESTAURANT, Level 41, Chifley Tower, 2 Chifley Street, Sydney, ph +61 (02) 9221 2500

LA MENSA, 257 Oxford Street, Paddington, Sydney, NSW 2021, ph +61 (02) 9332 2963

ROCKPOOL, 107 George Street, The Rocks, Sydney, ph +61 (02) 9252 1888

QUEENSLAND

CAIRNS GAME FISHING CLUB, Marlin Parade, Cairns, Qld 4870, ph +61 (07) 4031 5240

E'CCO LICENSED BISTRO, cnr Boundary & Adelaide Streets, Brisbane, Qld 4000, ph +61 (07) 3831 8344

FISHLIPS BAR & GRILL, 228 Sheridan Street, Cairns, Qld 4870, ph +61 (07) 4047 1700

IL CENTRO RESTAURANT & BAR, Shop 6, Eagle Street Pier, Brisbane, Qld 4000, ph +61 (07) 3221 6090

INDIGO BAR BISTRO, 695 Brunswick Street, New Farm, Qld 4005, ph +61 (07) 3254 0275

RED OCHRE GRILL, 43 Shields Street, Cairns, Qld 4870, ph +61 (07) 4051 0100

SIGGI'S, The Heritage Hotel, cnr Edward & Margaret Streets, Brisbane, ph +61 (07) 3221 4555

TABLES OF TOOWONG, 85 Miskin Street, Toowong, ph +61 (07) 3371 4558

TWO SMALL ROOMS, 817 Miton Road, Toowong, ph +61 (07) 3371 5251

ZEN BAR, Park Level, Post Office Square, 215 Adelaide Street, Brisbane, ph +61 (07) 3211 2333 — also at 55 Railway Terrace, Milton, Brisbane

VICTORIA

ADELPHI HOTEL, 187 Flinders Lane, Melbourne, Vic 3000, ph +61 (03) 9650 7555

BRIDPORT ONE-ONE-SIX, 116 Bridport Street, Albert Park, ph +61 (03) 9690 5155

FLOWER DRUM, 17 Market Lane, Melbourne, ph +61 (03) 9662 3655

GUERNICA RESTAURANT, 257 Brunswick Street, Fitzroy, Vic 3065, ph +61 (03) 9416 0969

IL BACARO, 168-170 Little Collins Street, Melbourne, Vic 3000, ph +61 (03) 9654 6778

ISIS, 10 Armstrong Street, Middle Park, Vic 3206, ph +61 (03) 9699 4244

MARCHETTI'S LATIN RESTAURANT, 55 Lonsdale Street, Melbourne, Vic 3000, ph +61 (03) 9662 1985

O'CONNELLS, 407 Coventry Street, South Melbourne, Vic 3205, ph +61 (03) 9699 9600

STELLA, 159 Spring Street, Melbourne, Vic 3000, ph +61 (03) 9639 1555

WESTERN AUSTRALIA

CABLE BEACH INTER-CONTINENTAL RESORT, Cable Beach Road, Broome, WA 6725, ph +61 (08) 9192 0400

COCO'S, cnr Mends Street & The Esplanade, South Perth, WA 6151, ph +61 (08) 9474 3030

FRASER'S RESTAURANT, Kings Park, West Perth, WA 6005, ph +61 (08) 9481 7100

JESSICA'S FINE SEAFOOD RESTAURANT, Shop 1, Hyatt Centre, 23 Plain Street, East Perth, ph +61 (08) 8232 3266

JOE'S ORIENTAL DINER, Hyatt Regency Perth, 99 Adelaide Terrace, Perth, WA 6000, ph +61 (08) 9225 1268

NO. 44 KING STREET, 44 King Street, Perth, WA 6000, ph +61 (08) 9321 4476

SOUTH AUSTRALIA

BOLTZ CAFÉ & BAR, 286 Rundle Street, Adelaide, ph +61 (08) 8232 5234

THE BOTANIC DINING ROOM, 309 North Terrace, Adelaide, SA 6000, ph +61 (08) 8232 3266

CAON'S, 19 Leigh Street, Adelaide, ph +61 (08) 8231 3011

DON'S TABLE, Shop 1, 136 The Parade, Norwood, SA 5067, ph +61 (08) 8364 3488

JOLLEYS BOATHOUSE RESTAURANT, Jolleys Lane, Adelaide, SA 5000, ph +61 (08) 223 2891

THE MANSE, 142 Tynte Street, North Adelaide, SA 5006, ph +61 (08) 8267 4636

THE OXFORD, 101 O'Connell Street, North Adelaide, SA 5006, ph +61 (08) 8267 2652

RED OCHRE GRILL, 129 Gouger Street, Adelaide, ph +61 (08) 8212 7266

UNIVERSAL WINE BAR, 285 Rundle Street, Adelaide, ph +61 (08) 8232 5000

TASMANIA

MURES UPPER DECK, Mures Fish Centre, Victoria Dock, Hobart, ph +61 (03) 6231 1999

PANACHE, 89 Salamanca Place, Hobart, ph +61 (03) 6224 2929

ROCKERFELLER'S, 11 Morrison Street, City Mill, Hobart, Tas 7000, ph +61 (03) 6234 3490

SYRUP, 1st Floor, 39 Salamanca Place, Hobart, Tas 7000, ph +61 (03) 6224 8249

NORTHERN TERRITORY

CORNUCOPIA MUSEUM CAFÉ, Bullocky Point, Canacher Street, Fannie Bay, NT 0801, ph +61 (08) 8981 1002

LINDSAY STREET CAFÉ LICENSED RESTAURANT, 2 Lindsay Street, Darwin, NT 0800, ph +61 (08) 8981 8631

RISTORANTE PUCCINI, Ansett Building, Todd Mall, Alice Springs, NT 0871, ph +61 (08) 8953 0935

AUSTRALIAN CAPITAL TERRITORY

FRINGE BENEFITS RESTAURANT & WINE BAR, 54 Marcus Clarke Street, Canberra City, ACT 2601, ph +61 (06) 247 4042

Turkey in Mole Poblano 124

Prawn, Mango & Wild Lime Timbale Salad 153
Pressed Terrine of Smoked Tomatoes on an Avocado Ratatouille & Warm
    Gympie Farm Goats' Cheese 168

RABBIT
Roast Crown of Hare on a Gateau of Cabbage & Oriental Mushrooms with a
    Cepe Mushroom Sauce 16

Rack of Lamb 'in Vogue' 186
Rare Peppered Salmon 164
Red Curry of Blue Manna Crab, Bok Choy & Jasmine Rice 136
Roast Crown of Hare on a Gateau of Cabbage & Oriental Mushrooms with a
    Cepe Mushroom Sauce 16
Roast Fillet of Biodynamic Beef with Potato Mash & Olive Purée 130
Roast Lamb Rack, Garlic Potatoes, Spinach & Mint Jus 132
Roast Split Marron 100
Roasted Garlic & Anchovy Bavarois with Octopus Aioli, Almond & Anchovy
    Tuille, Couscous & Parsley & a Beetroot & Saffron Dressing 126
Salad of Beetroot, Asparagus, Mache & Goats' Cheese 38
Salad of Roast Duck, Sea Scallops & Sichuan Pickled Cucumbers 18

SALADS
Prawn, Mango & Wild Lime Timbale Salad 153
Salad of Beetroot, Asparagus, Mache & Goats' Cheese 38
Salad of Roast Duck, Sea Scallops & Sichuan Pickled Cucumbers 18
Thai Beef Salad 119
Warm Salad of Smoked Eel & Southern Golds 64

Salmon Gravlax 134
Sautéed Crocodile Strips on Sweet Potato & Red Curry Fritters with Parsley &
    Pecan Nut Salsa 184
Sautéed Prawns & Roast Sweet Potato, Red Wine Reduction & Basil Oil 102
Scarola 63
Seafood Mosaique 182

SHELLFISH
Champagne Oysters 81
Coconut Prawns with Spiced Mango Chutney 141
Confit of Greenlip Abalone & Black Fungi, Noodle Salad & Truffle Oil
    Dressing 14
Hot & Sour Yabbies 114
Mud Crab Omelet 174
Oysters with Salsa of Mango, Cucumber & Chilli 116
Pan-fried Hervey Bay Scallops 162
Pink Peppercorn & Mustard Seed Marinade (for Pearl Meat) 148
Prawn, Mango & Wild Lime Timbale Salad 153
Red Curry of Blue Manna Crab, Bok Choy & Jasmine Rice 136
Roast Split Marron 100
Sautéed Prawns & Roast Sweet Potato, Red Wine Reduction & Basil Oil 102
Seafood Mosaique 182
Stir-fried Seafood with Ginger & Oyster Sauce 146

Smoked Salmon Layer Cake with Horseradish Cream 180
Smoked Salmon with Chilli Corncakes, Rocket & Soused Leeks 170
Snapper with Cannellini Beans & Truffle Oil 41

SOUPS
La Mensa's Jerusalem Artichoke Soup 24
Scarola 63

Spring Smoked Salmon & Passionfruit & Orange Dressing & Salad 113

STARTERS
Antipasto Del Bàcaro 56
Baked Figs with Gorgonzola Sauce 35
Cable Beach's Marinated Pearl Meat 148
Lambs' Brains with Hollandaise 106

Steamed Chinese Greens with Oyster Sauce 167
Stingray & Green Mango Salad with Crispy Fish 72
Stir-fried Seafood with Ginger & Oyster Sauce 146
Swordfish Steak with Kerala Curry 29
Tartare of Yellowfin Tuna with Beetroot Oil & Oscietre Caviar 42
Thai Beef Salad 119
Turkey in Mole Poblano 124
Turkish Coffee Ice Cream with Hazelnut Florentines & Fresh Berries 68
Vanilla Bean & Chocolate Brownie Ice-Cream Cake with Berries 86

VEGETABLE DISHES
Goats' Cheese & Eggplant Pastry Stack 96
Pressed Terrine of Smoked Tomatoes on an Avocado Ratatouille & Warm
    Gympie Farm Goats' Cheese 168
Steamed Chinese Greens with Oyster Sauce 167

VENISON
Onkaparinga Valley Venison with Red Currant Sauce 122

Warm Plum Galette 76
Warm Salad of Smoked Eel & Southern Golds 64
Whole Fried Salt & Pepper Barramundi with Stir-fried Bok Choy 110
Wild Lime Lamington 104

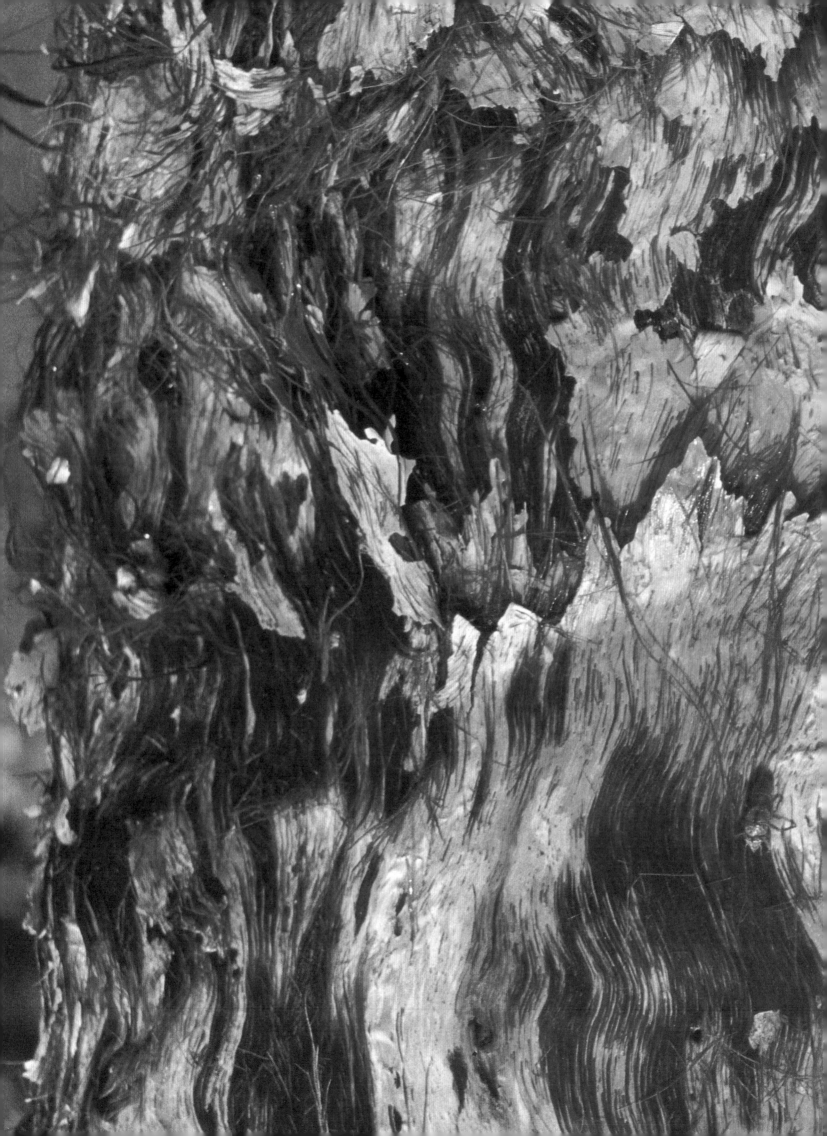